NOVA SCOTIA MOMENTS

Clary Croft

NIMBUS
PUBLISHING LTD

Nimbus Publishing Limited
PO Box 9166
Halifax, NS   B3K 5M8
(902) 455-4286

Printed and bound in Canada
Design: Kathy Kaulbach, Paragon Design Group
Author photo: Sharon Croft

Library and Archives Canada Cataloguing in Publication

Croft, Clary
Nova Scotia moments / Clary Croft.
Includes bibliographical references.
ISBN 1-55109-496-7

1. Nova Scotia--History--Miscellanea. I. Title.

FC2311.C76 2004   971.6'002   C2004-904791-4

We acknowledge the financial support of the Government of
Canada through the Book Publishing Industry Development
Program (BPIDP) and the Canada Council for our publishing
activities.

Table of Contents

Introduction

In 2002 I got a call from Jack McGaw inviting me to contribute a daily bit of Nova Scotian folklore and/or history for the fledgling Information Radio 97.9. Jack had recently retired to Nova Scotia after a busy and well-recognized career in television and, for some inexplicable reason, decided to jump headfirst into a new media adventure. I always assumed that retirement meant slowing down a bit, but Jack's commitment and dedication to making this resource for community news, reports and information a vital part of the life of the Halifax Regional Municipality is amazing. I'm delighted to be part of the team!

People often ask me where I dig up all this information. Well, for over thirty-five years, I have been reading and collecting information about my beloved home province, Nova Scotia. I rarely just read a book. Most often I have paper and pen handy and note the page where something tweaks my interest. Then I go back and enter the information in my data base. Unpublished archival sources are great fun. Some times I look for specific data; other times I just allow myself to roam at random—and I'm never disappointed. I guess you have to be a certain kind of person to ferret this stuff out—obsessive is such a strong word! But it's a passion, and when you are doing something you love, the concept of work doesn't enter the picture. My great fortune is that my passion just happens to be my work.

As the title of this books suggests, these are nothing more than brief glimpses into tiny aspects of Nova Scotia's history, culture and folk beliefs. No attempt has been made at in-depth study, although a selected bibliography has been provided. I like to think that one or more of these pieces may inspire the reader to investigate more about the items they find interesting. Many people tell me they enjoy my Nova Scotia Moments on 97.9. It's a way to connect to their home province. And for those of you less fortunate (and by that I mean you live elsewhere), I hope you enjoy learning something about this beautiful corner of the world and its fascinating and delightful people.

And, finally, my thanks:
To my colleagues at Information Radio 97.9: to Jack McGaw for asking me to contribute my daily Nova Scotia Moments and to Doug Barron and James MacLeod for the coffee and fun at the recording sessions.

Thanks to the folks at Nimbus Publishing: Sandra McIntyre, Heather Bryan, Penelope Jackson, Helen Matheson and Dan Soucoup.

To the folks who provided images: you're listed in the photo credits, but even a second "thank you" seems inadequate.

To the staff at the Nova Scotia Archives and Record Management and the Dartmouth Heritage Museum: my sincere gratitude for going beyond the normal call for information, especially in finding the graphics for this book.

To my family and friends: you make my life rich and full!

And, as always, to my darling Sharon. Because of you I am rich beyond measure!

Nova Scotia's population is a mélange of many cultures. Today's Nova Scotians can trace their origins to many different ethnic backgrounds and cultures. Naturally, the

A Diverse People

Mi'kmaq were here long before any recorded history, but for the first three hundred years of post-contact settlement, the majority of people inhabiting this area came from six cultural groups: Mi'kmaq, French (Acadians), English, Celts, Blacks and Germans. With the myriad of cultures present today there are, and will be, many more stories to tell. The following stories reflect those six early groups, and some of the others that followed.

• • • The **Maroons** were a band of escaped slaves and freedom fighters from Jamaica who were captured and brought to Nova Scotia. Approximately five hundred arrived in Halifax on July 22, 1796. It is said that the Duke of Kent employed many of the men in building a section of the fortress at Citadel Hill. Dissatisfied with inadequate living conditions and inaction by the government, many Maroons accepted an offer to relocate to Africa, to the new British colony of Sierra Leone. On August 8, 1800, the ship *Asia* embarked with most of the Maroons from Nova Scotia for the long sea voyage to Sierra Leone—the largest free migration of blacks in history. And even today, in some parts of Sierra Leone, ancestors of the Maroons from Nova Scotia will ask of their former homeland: "How are things in Scotia-land?" •

Claude Darrach, Herring Cove, one of the original crew members of *Bluenose*, standing in front of a photo of the famous schooner.

• • • Why are Nova Scotians called **Bluenoses**? It's not because of the famous racing schooner. The answer depends, in part, on the dictionary you consult. *The Dictionary of Canadianism* has traced the word back to 1785 when it was applied to the original inhabitants of Nova Scotia, in contrast to the United Empire Loyalists. But it was those Nova Scotians who were loyal to the crown—true blue—that helped perpetuate the name. Famed Nova Scotia writer Thomas Chandler Haliburton's fictional character, the Yankee peddler Sam Slick, reasoned that "it is the name of a potato which the [Nova Scotians] produce in great perfection and boast to be the best in the world. The Americans have, in consequence, given them the nickname of blue-noses." Others had different ideas. Sir Charles G. D. Roberts attributed the term to the fame of a legendary privateer vessel easily recognized by a blue cannon in the prow. Another theory, this one from Captain Randall Merrian of Bridgetown, suggests the nickname comes from New Englanders who, in the eighteenth century, used to sail to the Gulf Coast for cod. They used to stop off the south coast of Nova Scotia to catch herring for bait, the favoured species being the blue nose herring. Soon, smart Nova Scotians began catching the fish and selling it directly to the New Englanders, who would watch out for these bait-sellers whom they called the "bluenose" people. And finally, it has been suggested that the term arose when blue stain rubbed off from sailors' indigo-dyed sweaters when they wiped their noses on their sleeves. •

• • • Dartmouth was once home to a sizable **Quaker community** — Nantucket whalers who accepted an offer by the British government to settle in British territory when restrictions on whaling products were imposed by the United States. Ten vessels arrived in 1784, bringing approximately three hundred people along with supplies and homes ready to be reassembled on the new sites. They had a meeting house on the corner of King and Queen streets in a section once known as Quaker Town. However, they didn't stay long. English buyers of whale products wanted more control over the business so the community moved to Wales in 1792. The lives of Dartmouth's Quakers are illustrated at the Quaker House Museum, operated by the Dartmouth Heritage Museum Society. •

Quaker House, Dartmouth, Nova Scotia.

• • • In 1996 the Nova Scotia government proclaimed May **Gaelic Awareness Month**, and for good reason, when you consider the influence our Gaelic ancestors have had in the province and worldwide. In fact, the first Gaelic newspaper in the world was published not in Scotland or Ireland, but right here in Nova Scotia. On May 28, 1892, the *Mac Talla* (The Echo) was published in Sydney by Jonathan G. MacKinnon of Dunakin, near Whycocomagh. It carried local and world news, as well as history, proverbs, Greek

mythology and correspondence. Its tenure was short-lived, however, lasting a mere dozen years. The newspaper was published for the last time on June 24, 1904.

Many early Celtic settlers to Nova Scotia claimed Gaelic as their mother tongue. The language was included in the national census for the first time in 1931 and of the 32,000 Gaelic-speaking people living in Canada, 24,000 were living in Nova Scotia, with the majority in Cape Breton. In the early part of World War II, the Canadian Board of Censors foolishly included Gaelic as one of the languages banned on public radio stations and in telephone conversations as a wartime security measure. The authorities rescinded the ban after a great public outcry from Cape Breton Gaelic communities.

We tend to think of Pictou County and parts of Cape Breton as the bastions of Gaelic language in the province. That may be so now, but eighteenth-century Halifax was once so full of Gaelic speakers that in 1756 people spoke of "Wild Irish" or Gaelic as one of the most common dialects in town. •

• • • When the American colonies rebelled against Great Britain, thousands of people loyal to the crown fled to Nova Scotia. But some of the **United Empire Loyalists** to arrive in 1783 were quickly dissatisfied with the way the government treated the king's loyal subjects. A popular verse in Shelburne was:

> **On Scotia's barren rocky shore**
> **Consign'd to labour and be poor;**
> **For what the king in bounty gave**
> **Half serv'd to poor, half kept by knave.** •

• • • Halifax's Pier 21, Canada's national symbol of the **immigrant experience**, is a wonderful museum full of tales of hope and dreams come true. But the story has its dark side too: Not everyone was treated as an equal. A 1926 brochure titled *Eastern Canada*, issued by the federal Minister of Immigration and Colonization, carried the following admonishment in a section called "Useful Information for Settlers": "All women unaccompanied by husband, father, or mother coming to Canada to engage in housework or industrial employment must receive an emigration permit and travel in a conducted party." •

• • • Nova Scotia was once home to a large **Icelandic population**. The government of Nova Scotia sent agents to Iceland in the 1870s to entice settlers to the province. In 1875, seventeen families from Iceland settled Mooseland Heights, inland from Tangier, in Halifax County. It was renamed Markland in their honour. In 1877, 1878 and 1879 the group was joined by other families, and by 1880 the total population of Icelandic settlers had reached two hundred persons, including several families in Lockeport. However, by 1882 news of a land boom in Winnipeg and free land in Dakota caused all but a few of the settlers to pull up stakes and relocate. •

• • • **Chinese immigration** to Nova Scotia has had a long and rocky history. The 1891 census for Nova Scotia lists only five Chinese, mainly in the Halifax/Dartmouth area. Chinese had to be sponsored to get into Canada and had to pay a head tax. Then the Exclusion Act, which was enacted in 1923, stopped Chinese immigration completely, and was not repealed until 1947.

Because of prejudice, few work opportunities were open to Chinese except in the food service and laundry industries. Mr. N. Lee was one of the first Chinese in Halifax when he arrived from China in 1903. He opened a laundry on Bliss Street in 1910 and it wasn't until 1919 that his wife was permitted to join him. The last Chinese laundry in Halifax (and perhaps in Nova Scotia) closed down in 1978 when Charles Wong and his wife retired. Robert Doyle, then head of the Costume Studies Program at Dalhousie University, made sure some of the equipment from the Wongs' shop was saved; it now forms part of our national heritage collection at the Canadian Museum of Civilization in Ottawa. •

Tuesday, July 2, 1935

Brilliant Spectacle Is Provided By Youth

SIR Robert Baden-Powell giving his address to the assembled Scouts at the Dalhousie campus yesterday afternoon, and speaking into the microphone of the loud speaker system installed for the occasion. In front is seen the Chief Guide's colors, and the party acting as special color guard.

Sir Baden Powell's visit to Halifax, Nova Scotia, 1935. *Halifax Mail*, July 2, 1935.

• • • The towns of Merrickville, Ontario, and Port Morien, Nova Scotia, vie for the bragging rights of being the first place in Canada to have a **Boy Scout troop**. The general nod seems to go to Port Morien which began Scouting activities in 1908, less than a year after the original organization was started in England by Baden Powell. Today, there are more than three hundred Scouting groups in Nova Scotia, with more than 16,000 members including Beavers, Cubs, Scouts, Venturers and Rovers. These young people have been doing good deeds for years. The Boy Scouts of Canada was one of the first organizations to foster interest in recycling programs. Scouts are encouraged to aim for at least one good deed every day. For Halifax's bicentennial celebrations in 1949, Scouts planted thousands of trees in the city's watershed, many of which are still standing. Good deed Scouts! •

• • • Some traditional Nova Scotian folk tales can be traced to their **African origins**. In his 1931 publication, *Folklore from Nova Scotia*, folk collector Arthur Huff Faucet found several African Nova Scotians who told traditional African "Anancy" tales. Anancy, the trickster in African stories, is commonly called Nancy in the versions found in this province. One such tale, told by Jerry Paris of New Glasgow, explains why Dog is so slim around the middle.

One day Nancy and Dog went to pick apples. Dog told Nancy he was too big to climb the tree so Nancy climbed up and threw the apples down to Dog. Naturally as fast as Nancy threw the apples down, Dog ate them, and when Nancy came down from the tree he discovered not only that Dog had eaten all the apples but that he was hiding headfirst in a hole he had dug to escape Nancy's wrath. But Dog was so bloated from the apples he couldn't get all the way in the hole. Nancy grabbed Dog around the waist and hauled him out. And, as Jerry Paris said, "That's what makes Dog so slim aroun' the band." •

• • • We Nova Scotians have a reputation for overusing the word **some**:

"That chocolate cake is some good".

"He's some lazy".

"That's some beautiful boat you got there".

Apparently, the use of the word is a holdover from British speech patterns. According to University of New Brunswick linguist Murray Queenlike, the same word usage is found in Britain, especially around Cornwall, Lincolnshire and Lancashire. That's right some interesting, isn't it? •

• • • **Slavery** was officially abolished in the British Empire in 1833, an act that merited little news in the local popular press of the day. The *Nova Scotian* of August 28, 1833, contains a small entry in the "General News" section—a mention that the Slavery Opposition Bill in Britain's parliament had been agreed upon. However, the people it most affected were those who just a day earlier had been enslaved. On the day of freedom, the congregation of the African chapel on Cornwallis Street in Halifax, led by the Reverend Richard Preston, sang this spiritual:

Sound the loud timbrels o'er Egypt's dark sea, Jehovah hath triumphed his people are free. •

• • • The most visible symbol of **Acadian pride** in Nova Scotia is the tricolour red, white and blue flag with the bright yellow star—the Acadian flag! The design was chosen during the Second National Acadian Convention in Miscouche, Prince Edward Island, in 1884. It was proposed by the Reverend Marcel-François Richard from Saint-Louis, New Brunswick. He told members of the congress that "the tricoloured flag is France's flag, of which we are descendants, and this flag has the right to fly throughout the entire universe according to international laws. For us, Acadians, this flag simply tells us that we are French and that France is our motherland, just like the Irish flag reminds the Irish of their origin and homeland. However, I would like Acadia to have a flag which would remind us not only that our children are French, but that they are Acadian...The tricoloured flag...would represent Acadia, since a yellow star would be added to the blue section. The star, representing the star of Mary, Stella Maris, would serve as a crest in the Acadian flag, the same way the Union Jack was used as a crest in the Canadian confederation flag...." •

Acadian flag flying at Province House, in celebration of the 400th Anniversary of Acadian settlement in Nova Scotia, 2004.

• • • From the late 1860s until the late 1940s, between 80,000 and 100,000 **British Home Children** were sent to Canada by more than fifty British childcare organizations. Many poor families had their children removed with the promise they would have a better life in Canada; it was also an opportunity for many organizations to rid themselves of illegitimate or orphaned children. While most of these children were shipped off to Upper and Western Canada, hundreds of Home Children were sent to the Daykene Farm in Falmouth, Nova Scotia. Many of the younger children were adopted and had good homes, although a substantial number of the older children were used as a cheap form of farm labour and suffered terrible lives. It is estimated that twenty percent of Canadians can trace their roots to a Home Child. •

• • • This quote may fall under the category

If you can't say something nice about someone, don't say anything at all.

In the eighteenth century an evangelical fervor sometimes called **The New Light Movement** swept through the eastern seaboard. One of the movement's chief preachers, Henry Alline, paid a visit to Halifax in January of 1783. To say the least, he wasn't impressed. He wrote in his journal, "The people in general are almost as dark and as vile as in Sodom." •

• • • A good number of Nova Scotians can trace part of their ancestry back to **Ireland**, but throughout the province's early history, the Irish were not always the most favoured citizens. They may have had numbers on their side, but they had to cope with religious and social prejudices. The first federal census of 1871 shows that the Irish held the majority in the capital, Halifax, with almost 39 percent of the population claiming origins in the Old Sod. They were followed by the English at almost 33 percent, Scots at 16 percent, Germans near 5 percent, Africans at slightly more than 2 percent and the French at 1.6 percent. •

• • • The first recorded **Jewish settler** to Halifax was Isaac Solomon, who arrived with his Christian wife and two daughters in 1750. By 1752, there were approximately thirty individuals in the fledgling town identified as Jews. In those early days Jewish religious services were held in homes and, for the most part, Jews kept a low profile. The 1871 federal census lists no Jews in the province, while the Nova Scotia census of that year lists less than thirty. In the 1890s, a small group of Halifax Jews formed the Baron de Hirsh Benevolent Society, bought the former Christian church on Starr Street and opened the city's first synagogue. •

Jewish Synagogue, Halifax, 1896.

• • • In 1896, **Rudyard Kipling** published *Captains Courageous*, a classic novel with several unforgettable literary characters. One of these fictional characters was actually based on a Nova Scotian, or perhaps I should say, two Nova Scotians—twin brothers from Cape Breton. Kipling's story is a tale of a young rich lad swept overboard from a luxury vessel, only to be picked up by a Grand Banks fishing schooner. One of the workers on that schooner, a Black cook, was modelled after twins George and John Maxwell. An outstanding feature in the story is that this cook speaks Gaelic, then considered a rare language for someone of African heritage. Kipling wrote, "His natural tongue's kinder curious. Comes from the innards of Cape Breton…where the farmers speak homemade Scotch…." The real Cape Breton Gaelic-speaking African Nova Scotians were the sons of a Black Loyalist raised by a Gaelic-speaking family. Both men were known to be fine singers and composed songs in Gaelic. •

• • • The settlers known as **Foreign Protestants** came to Nova Scotia beginning in 1750, with the majority eventually settling along the south shore of the province. My own ancestor, Johann "Jacob" Kraft (the family name was changed to Croft in the 1830s), arrived on the ship *Ann* in 1750, and with his second wife, Anna Maria Ramichen, helped found the town of Lunenburg. These settlers came from various areas of middle Europe including Germany, Switzerland and France. The early days were hard as reported by Anna Mossman of Rose Bay to Helen Creighton: "They used to get letters from home [i.e. Germany] but they never answered them…they said if they'd write back and say how hard it was, the families would say they told them so; but if they told them everything was fine, they might come over and really find out the truth for themselves." •

• • • As they often are today, **Mi'kmaw feasts** were more than occasions for dining—they were also opportunities for passing on oral traditions and customs. After the meal it was customary to bring out a tobacco pipe and share it with the elders and guests. While some pipe bowls were made from stone, a frequent receptacle for the smouldering indigenous tobacco was a lobster claw attached to a long wooden stem. It would first be lit by the chief or oldest male present and then a speech would be made to the host after which the pipe would be circulated to the remaining male guests. This ritual was followed by storytelling, singing, and feats of oration. •

Mi'kmaw Encampment near Halifax, Nova Scotia 1812.

Crime and Punishment

The perception of the severity of illegal or criminal activities often depends upon the morals of the society in which they are committed. The same holds true for the punishments. In eighteenth-century Nova Scotia, petty crimes such as stealing were dealt with in a far harsher way than they are today. What was once deemed socially abhorrent by many is now an accepted norm. You be the judge.

In eighteenth- and early nineteenth-century Nova Scotia, if a man was walking down the street and heard the cry of **"Press!"** he ran as fast as he could for safety. This method of enforced enlistment was common in Nova Scotia, especially during the Napoleonic Wars and the War of 1812. Sanctioned by the British Admiralty, press gangs would be allowed twenty-four hours to "recruit," which usually meant hitting someone over the head and carrying him on board ship or to a detention centre for later shipment. Either way,

you're in His Majesty's Service, fella, and you'd better learn to like it. •

Melville Island looking towards the head of the North West Arm showing the prison, c.1888.

Halifax was once home to a fascinating **island prison**. Edward Cornwallis called the island in the North West Arm "Sandwich Island". Later, it was known as Cowie's or Kavanaugh's Island, and finally, in 1804, the British Admiralty named it Melville Island. It was first used as a prison in 1803 during the Napoleonic Wars, and later, during the War of 1812. It was said that the prisoners didn't try to escape because the guards kept a pet shark swimming around the island with regular feedings. During the Napoleonic era, citizens from Halifax would travel to the prison for an afternoon's amusement. There the prisoners would set up shop in a market atmosphere and sell toothpicks, combs, dominoes, and intricate ships' models made from soup bones and rigged with human hair. •

• • • Today's criminals get off a lot lighter than their counterparts in early Nova Scotia. In 1734, Sett Matthew Hurry of Annapolis Royal stole three pounds from James Thomson and received fifty lashes on his bare back with a **cat-o'-nine tails**. In 1827 John Maser received one year hard labour for stealing a pair of shoes. And in 1855 several young lads in Halifax were fined twenty shillings or ten days at hard labour for robbing from the lieutenant-governor's apple trees. •

• • • One of the most interesting forms of **credit** for many early Nova Scotians was the bill they were allowed to run up at the company store. Mining and logging operations were notorious for allowing their employees to get credit at their establishments. Most times it was the employees' only option. When it came time to pay off their chit, many workers found they owed more than they made. Perhaps that's the reason some of these establishments were referred to as "the pluck me store." •

• • • In its early years, Halifax didn't have a specific **building for prisoners**. The first prisons were on ships in the harbour. Stockades and cells were found ashore in any dwelling that could be made secure. In 1784, Joseph Ford returned from the siege of Louisbourg to find the government had taken over his house to use as a jail. He had no other recourse but to allow them to stay. The orders came directly from Governor Lawrence, and Mr. Ford was to receive no compensation. His objections were useless as military law was in force. •

• • • In eighteenth- and nineteenth-century Nova Scotia, people unable to pay their bills were put in **debtors' prisons** until they could pay off their debts. That meant it was left to family and friends to pay off what was owed. Although many jails had a specific room for special debtors, they were far from luxurious. Many rooms in the jail were without fireplaces, and a report to the provincial government in 1819 stated that "spiritous liquors are sold by the jailor to the prisoners in such quantities as to cause riot and drunkenness—this should be stopped." One has to ask—if a person was in jail for debts and couldn't pay his way out, how did he find money to buy booze from the guards? •

• • • Before the twentieth century, **dueling**, although not common, was certainly one option for settling a dispute in Nova Scotia. Some duels ended in death, while others had happier endings. In 1801, an army officer stationed at Sydney, Cape Breton, challenged his friend to a duel. They met, faced each other with pistols, walked thirty paces away, turned and fired. To the horror of the onlookers, both men fell to the ground with the breasts of their white shirts stained crimson. Then, in a perhaps even more frightening sequel, both men stood up: Their seconds had substituted the shot with a mixture of gunpowder and cranberries. •

• • • The movement to abolish the sale and use of **liquor** began in the late 1820s and soon engulfed most of North America. The Bear River Temperance Hall, established 1828, is said to be the oldest in Nova Scotia. However, the West River, Pictou County division, also established in 1828, disputes the Bear River claim. Temperance leagues did a great deal of relief work in aid of destitute families. Societies held public meetings with testimonies about the dangers of drink and methods to avoid spirits. They also collected funds and sold goods to aid in their efforts. Perhaps the oddest expenditure was made by a branch in Antigonish where their books show the purchase of

Temperance paper *Social Reformer*, December 22, 1886.

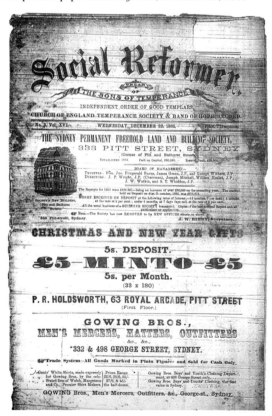

liquor at auction. The liquor was destroyed to prevent it from getting into the wrong hands. •

• • • Prohibition was a boon time for Nova Scotians who took up the trade of **rum-running**. Many vessels from the province were involved in smuggling booze from St. Pierre and Miquelon and various ports on the Caribbean into the eastern United States and Canada. The usual deal was for the Nova Scotian vessel to meet a fast cutter coming out of an American port and offload the cargo outside the twelve-mile limit. Then the cutter would race for the shore. The men had signals with playing cards, or, more commonly, half-dollar bills. The mother ship would match the cards or serial numbers on the bills with those of the cutters to verify a friendly and safe encounter. •

• • • Near the present Victoria General Hospital, site of the Queen Elizabeth II health complex, stands one of Halifax's old **hanging grounds**. In 1924, an article in the *Acadian Recorder* carried a first-hand account of the execution of mutineers and murderers from the ship *Saladan* which took place on July 30, 1844. The eyewitness quoted in the article, Mr. Forhan, was six years old at the time of the executions. He stood with his father and mother on the Victoria General Hospital site and saw two wagons carrying the condemned men from the penitentiary. They were accompanied by a squad of soldiers with fixed bayonets. They came up Tower Road, and, when two hundred yards from the spot where the gallows were erected, the troops formed a circle around the wagon. Mr. Forhan said, "This was the exact spot, and after they dropped we started for home, and on top of the Citadel, looking back, saw the heads of the four men still hanging on the gallows." •

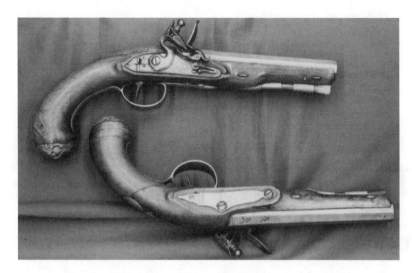

Pair of pistols, with silver decoration, marked "J. Richards."

• • • James Johnston and Charles Fairbanks were **lawyers** practising in Halifax in 1845. During a trial, Johnston offended Fairbanks and a duel was set to take place off Spring Garden Road. Tradition states that Fairbanks fired first and missed. Then Johnston aimed at Fairbanks' foot and said, "I will stop you dancing!" He fired and shot his opponent's heel. But afterwards, they became the best of friends. In fact, when Mr. Fairbanks died, his son told how his father's former dueling opponent came and wept with his widow over the loss of the man who had become his great friend. •

Famous Folks

Fame is subjective.

Some seek it; others have it find them.
Some attain international renown; others
have their celebrity blaze then extinguish
into relative obscurity. Some contribute to
society; others reap the bulk of the benefits
for themselves. One thing is certain: history
applauds success but can easily ignore good
deeds done by ordinary folks.

• • • **Alexander Graham Bell** was a long-time resident of Nova Scotia. His father-in-law, Gardiner Hubbard, was a Boston businessman who had a financial interest in the Caledonia mine field at Glace Bay in Cape Breton. On a visit to the mine in 1877, Mr. Hubbard brought two of his son-in-law's new inventions with him and installed a telephone line running down the shaft—the first use of the telephone in Nova Scotia and the first use of the system underground anywhere in the world. •

Alexander Graham Bell seated in a tetrahedral chair. August 12, 1907.

• • • **Susannah and John Oland** came from England to Nova Scotia in the mid-1860s. John, an accountant, was to work for the Intercolonial Railway, but by 1867, he was out of a job. Susannah was known for her fine homemade beer, and a friend recommended they make the brew for the military. They got a contract and began the Army and Navy Brewing Company. In 1877, Susannah changed the company name to Oland Sons and Company. The rest, as they say, is history! Oland's beer is still one of Nova Scotia's most popular brews. •

• • • Born in Scotland, **Sir Sanford Fleming** was the man responsible for developing the world's time zones in 1885. Sir Sanford lived for several years in a house on Brunswick Street in Halifax, and he also had an estate on the beautiful North West Arm. In 1908, the Nova Scotia Legislative Assembly was one hundred years old, making it the oldest parliament in the Empire next to the British Parliament. To celebrate this event, Sir Sanford donated a huge part of his estate on the Arm, to be known as Fleming Park. He worked with other countries in the Empire to erect a memorial tower, which was dedicated on August 12, 1912. The park, with its handsome stone tower, is still a popular recreation area for Haligonians. •

• • • Born in 1885 at Welsford in Nova Scotia's Annapolis Valley, **Albert Fuller** moved to Boston at age eighteen. After trying his hand at various odd jobs, he bought a fifteen-dollar hand-operated wire-twister and went into the business of making brushes. He eventually moved to Hartford and set up a factory to run the business he called The Capital Brush Company. However, since another company already had that name, he used his own, and The Fuller Brush Company was born.

Albert built the most successful door-to-door business in American and Canadian history. His life and career even made it to the silver screen. In 1948 Hollywood made the movie *The Fuller Brush Man* starring Lucille Ball and featuring Red Skelton in the title role. The Nova Scotia movie premiere was held in Yarmouth. Albert attended and handed out more than 450 brushes. He died in 1973 at age eighty-eight, leaving an estate worth 1.9 million—the world's wealthiest traveling salesman. •

• • • A nineteenth-century Nova Scotia farmer named **Charles Fennerty** should have made earlier claim to inventing pulp paper. One story is that he realized the process of making paper from wood fibres by watching wasps build their nests. Using the wasps as inspiration, he composed a paper from spruce wood reduced to pulp. By 1838, he had developed a workable paper. He wrote to the owner and publisher of the *Acadian Recorder* saying, "I entertain an opinion that our forests' trees ... on account of the fibrous quality of the woods, might easily be reduced by chafing, and manufactured into paper of the finest kind." Unfortunately, he discovered the process sixteen years before he announced it and then waited to make his claim two decades after the process was used commercially in Europe. One of the few tangible acknowledgments of his discovery is a tablet and stone cairn which stands to his memory in Sackville, his home community just outside Halifax. •

• • • An African Nova Scotian entrepreneur may hold the claim as the first policewoman in Canada. Early in the nineteenth century, **Rose Fortune**, a child of United Empire Loyalists, operated a carting business at the wharves of Annapolis Royal. She used a large wheelbarrow to transport trunks and baggage from ships to waiting carriages. Rose was a shrewd businesswoman who apparently tolerated no abuse. She is reputed to have appointed herself police-woman, and held the position for most of her adult life—perhaps Canada's, or North America's, first policewoman. •

• • • The Five Fishermen restaurant on Halifax's Argyle Street was once the home of the National School, the oldest school building still standing in the city. Later it became the Victorian School of Art and Design. This school was founded in the late 1880s under the initiative of **Anna Leonowens**, the "Anna" in *Anna and the King of Siam*. The Victorian School of Art and Design, which eventually became known as the Nova Scotia College of Art and Design, has garnered an international reputation for turning out highly qualified artists and designers. •

Portrait of Anna Leonowens by Robert Harris

Anna Swan and her husband, Captain Martin V. Bates

• • • Nova Scotia is the birthplace of one of the world's most famous giants. **Anna Swan** was born in 1846 at Mill Brook, Colchester County, but later moved to Tatamagouche. At the age of four, Anna was four feet six inches; at the age of seven, she was taller than her mother, and she eventually reached the height of seven feet, nine inches. For years she was a main attraction at P.T. Barnum's Museum in New York. In 1871, Anna met and married Captain Martin van Buren Bates, a man more than seven feet eight inches tall. They were married in a well-publicized ceremony in London, had several audiences with Queen Victoria, and traveled extensively for a number of years as "the largest married couple in the world." Anna's life and career are celebrated each year during the Anna Swan days in Tatamagouche. •

Tom Miller

• • • The first African Canadian in eastern Canada to be elected alderman was from Nova Scotia. **Tom Miller** was born in Halifax in 1917 and later worked at Sydney Steel in Cape Breton, at that time one of the few places where African Nova Scotians could earn equal pay. After serving in World War II, he won a seat on the Sydney council in 1955 and held that position for seventeen years. Tom Miller's memory lives on in the Tom Miller Human Rights Award presented to a deserving citizen by the Cape Breton Regional Municipality—a fitting memorial to a remarkable African Canadian citizen. •

• • • Canada's most famous multiple births were the Dionne quintuplets, born in Corbeil, Ontario, on May 24, 1934. But Nova Scotia already had its own set of quintuplets. On February 15, 1880, **Mr. and Mrs. Adam Murray** of Little Egypt, a tiny community about four miles from New Glasgow, added to their family of seven children by bringing five more into the world. Unfortunately, unlike the Dionnes, none of the Murray children lived beyond three days. A local photographer, J. R. Fraser, took two photographs of the children—one before the last child died and one after all five children were dead. The photographs were displayed in a local store window. Fearing their dead children would be turned into nothing more than a curiosity (it was reputed that a "Yankee" showman offered the parents money for permission to display the bodies) the parents buried the children in the cellar under their house and, three months later, reburied them in a secret location. Had the quintuplets lived, they could have been the world's most famous multiple births. Now we don't even know the location of their final resting place—and that's the way their parents wanted it. •

• • • Superheroes and great comic strip characters owe a lot to Canadian imagination. In the 1920s and '30s, hero comics were all the rage. Perhaps the most popular was a Canadian's concept of the ideal space alien. Toronto's Joe Schuster created Superman—the ultimate action hero. Closer to home, we have **Hal Foster**, the man who created the famous *Prince Valiant* cartoon series. Harold R. Foster was born in Halifax on August 18, 1892. He became an illustrator in the 1920s and in 1931 began illustrating the popular *Tarzan* syndicated comics. Then, in 1937, he premiered his own hero, Prince Valiant. Foster continued to draw the brave prince until 1971 when he relinquished the drawing work to another artist. He died in 1981. Another cartoon pioneer was also born in Nova Scotia. James R. Williams was born in Halifax, and when an infant, moved to Ohio. He went on to create one of the longest-running feature cartoons carried in syndicated papers throughout North America. He called it *Out Our Way*. •

Jim Williams' first cartoon for *Out Our Way* March 20, 1922.

The *Silver Dart*, being readied for take-off, 1909.

• • • The first woman in Nova Scotia, and perhaps the world, to fly in an airplane was **Dolly Macleod**. On October 7, 1909, Mrs. Macleod and her family and friends gathered to watch the famous *Silver Dart* land at the new aerodrome park at Baddeck Bridge. After he landed, the pilot, Casey Baldwin, asked if any of the women in attendance wished to go aloft.

Dolly jumped at the opportunity. The flight was short; she later said, "We circled around within a radius of about three miles, and I was back on the ground before many of them realized I had gone." It was her first—and last—flight! •

• • • **Peggy Standring** was the first female licensed pilot in Nova Scotia. She earned her wings in 1931, flying a Gypsy Moth at the Halifax Flying Club, which had a runway at the Halifax Airport off Chebucto Road. In order to qualify for her test, Peggy had to complete nine hours of flight instruction and pass the Royal Air Force medical exam. She had to wear a leather jacket, helmet and goggles, and on her maiden solo flight her instructor told her she came in like a drunken sailor. •

Peggy Richard [Standring], seated on wing, CF CDQ, in hanger, Halifax Airport, Chebucto Road, May 1931.

Duke of Kent

Madame St. Laurent

• • • When Queen Victoria's father, **Edward Duke of Kent**, lived in Halifax with his companion, **Julie St. Laurent**, they were said to have entered into a morganic marriage. (That's a marriage between a royal and a commoner, with the understanding that their children did not have rights to the royal's title.) It has long been rumoured that part of the legacy Edward and Julie left in Halifax was two children—a girl and a boy named Mary and John. The children went by the last name of Rees, which was probably the name of the family in Halifax that brought them up. The girl was said to have married a Halifax gentleman, and the boy lived in Mahone Bay under an upturned boat, and lived to an old age. •

Judge
Haliburton,
circa 1890.

• • • The first person to conduct an in-depth study of African Nova Scotian folklore was an African American scholar, **Arthur Huff Fauset**. He travelled throughout the province in 1925 and collected a wide range of lore from various areas, mainly communities with a predominantly African Nova Scotian population. He expressed surprise in the numbers of people of African heritage to be found here and added, "Most of us are accustomed to think that Negroes are not to be met in large numbers after one goes north of Boston." His work was published in the *Journal of the American Folklore Society* in 1931 and is a valuable resource for African Nova Scotian folklore today. •

• • • **Thomas Chandler Haliburton**, who was born at Windsor in 1796 and educated at King's College, is one of Nova Scotia's most famous authors. *The Literary History of Canada* suggests that in his day, he rivalled Dickens in popularity. His most lasting and influential work, first published in 1836, was titled *The Clockmaker: the Sayings and Doings of Sam Slick of Slickville*. It was through the words of the "Yankee" peddler Sam that Haliburton was able to poke fun at the Bluenoses. Many of Sam's folksy sayings are now part of every day North American speech:

"seeing is believing"; "it's raining cats and dogs"; "quick as a wink"; "stick-in-the mud"; and "the early bird gets the worm."•

• • • **Margaret Marshall Saunders** was born at Liverpool, Nova Scotia, in 1861. She had many pets as a child, and at age fifteen began to write stories, often about the animals she loved. When the American Humane Education Society put out a call for an inspirational story about dog welfare, Ms. Saunders entered the contest and won the two-hundred-dollar prize with a story modelled after an abused dog she knew that lived with her friends in Ontario. She called the story *Beautiful Joe: the Autobiography of a Dog* and published it using her last two names—Marshall Saunders, because she thought it sounded more masculine and might give her an edge with the judges. By 1894, she had a hit—the first Canadian writer to sell more than a million copies of a book • .

Margaret
Marshall
Saunders

• • • **William Robert Wolseley Winniett** was born at Annapolis, Nova Scotia, in 1773 or 1774 and entered the British Royal Navy at age eleven. In 1818 he began work on vessels off the coast of Africa in the suppression of, or at least the attempt to control, the slave trade. In 1845 he was appointed lieutenant-governor of the Gold Coast—present-day Ghana. He worked hard trying to halt the slave trade and in 1849 was knighted for his work, which was cited "to be vastly beneficial in suppressing the nefarious traffic in Africa, known all over the world as the slave trade." In 1851, a monument was erected in Africa to his memory, yet few Nova Scotians even know of his accomplishments. •

• • • **Enos Collins** led an extraordinary life. He was born at Liverpool, Nova Scotia, in 1774, went to sea as a cabin boy, and rose to the rank of captain before he was twenty. By 1799 he was made first lieutenant of the privateer vessel *Charles Mary Wentworth* and began making his fortune. He moved to Halifax at age thirty-seven where he dealt in shipping, banking, insurance, real estate, and privateering, including owning major shares in the most famous of all privateer ships working out of Nova Scotia: *Liverpool Packet*. In 1825, he and several other merchants formed the Halifax Banking Company, which became known as Collin's Bank because it was housed in his warehouse, (now part of Halifax's Historic Properties). By the time he had reached his nineties, Enos Collins was reputed to be the richest man in British North America, worth an estimated six million dollars. But he also had a reputation for being tight with his money. When a coach left his estate to take guests back to town, he always directed it to come back via the Halifax Hotel to pick up swill for his pigs. •

Enos Collins

• • • **Viola Desmond** is sometimes called "Nova Scotia's Rosa Parks." A successful African Nova Scotian businesswoman, Viola ran a beauty business and school. Known for her poise and professional manner, she was also admired for her business acumen. On November 8, 1946, she was stranded in New Glasgow when her car broke down en route from Halifax to Sydney. She went to the Roseland movie theatre and requested a downstairs ticket. Unaware of the "unwritten rule" that people of colour sit in the balcony only, she refused to change her seat, and the police came and removed her from the theatre and took her to jail. She was encouraged to take the issue to the recently formed Nova Scotia Association for the Advancement of Coloured People—the NSAACP. With their help, she took her case to the Supreme Court, but lost. However, her cause has been lauded as the "first known [court] challenge brought by a black woman in Canada against a racial segregation law." •

• • • Many people claim that **Dr. Archibald Huntsman** was the inventor of a process that began the huge frozen fish industry. Dr. Huntsman worked for the Biological Board of Canada in Halifax during the 1920s and created what he called an "ice-fillet"—a frozen portion of fish suitable for the commercial market. His process helped develop the east coast fishing industry and allowed fishermen to freeze fillets on their boats at sea. This innovation is said to have inspired Mr. Birdseye in the United States and it is his name that is usually associated with commercial frozen foods. But I wonder if Mr. Birdseye has an award named in his honour? Mr. Huntsman does! The Huntsman Award was created to honour our local inventor and an annual international award that recognizes contributors to oceanography, marine geosciences, and marine biology is awarded in Dr. Archibald Huntsman's name. •

• • • The *Halifax Morning Chronicle* of July 15, 1868, carried the following notice: "[The] Eureka washing machine, invented by a young man in Kings Co. in 1866, is for sale at A. Stephen & Son, our agents in Halifax." Unfortunately, the paper neglected to reveal the young man's name. Fortunately, we do know the names of some of our province's other inventors. A fellow by the name of **Thomas Robson** invented a self-acting fog bell in 1857. And **Fred Creed**, a morse code operator from Mill Village, invented a system for sending printed word messages using a typewriter adapted to produce punched strips of paper. In 1848 he sold his invention to the British Post Office and the Great Northern Telegraph Company, changing forever the world of communications. •

• • • Scientific and technological innovations certainly don't take a back seat in Nova Scotia. **J. Cameron Mackie** of Sydney was a metallurgist who contributed greatly to the international railway industry. Early steel rails used to develop splits, causing damage and wrecks. Mr. Mackie developed a slow cool method of steel production, and by 1940, most of the western world was employing this method to produce steel rails. Another success happened in 1967 when **Dr. Ian Henderson** of Halifax introduced a device permitting fast and safe recharging of long-life nickel-cadmium batteries. Still, not every invention hit the mark. In 1843 **Richard McFarlane** of Halifax applied for a patent and funding from the government. He wrote in his petition that he "respectfully sheweth that your petitioner has invented [a] perpetual motion or self-acting principle that can be made to operate with power sufficient to propel machinery." •

William Roue

• • • Famed naval architect **William Roue**, long a resident of Dartmouth, lived and had his studio at what is now 23 James Street. During World War II, American general Dwight D. Eisenhower declared that Roue-designed sectional barges were "the best ones of all." But the most famous of Mr. Roue's designs, destined to become fabled in Canadian history, was the fishing schooner *Bluenose*. Check your pockets—do you have a dime? The image of the schooner depicted on the reverse is based on the *Bluenose*. You're carrying around a piece of Dartmouth's and Canada's proud maritime history! •

• • • **Thomas Head Raddall** was born in England in 1903 and immigrated to Halifax in 1913. By 1918 he was working as a wireless operator at various telegraphic stations, and eventually served several stints on Sable Island. At these lonely outposts he began writing, drawing from local stories and people for his inspiration. In 1938, he quit his job as a bookkeeper and accountant at the Mersey Paper Company to devote his time to writing. He became one of Canada's most popular authors, producing more than seventeen books, many of which would become Canadian classics, including *Roger Sudden*, *His Majesty's Yankees*, *Halifax: Warden of the North*, *The Nymph and the Lamp*, *The Governor's Lady*, and *Hangman's Beach*. I met Tom several times and during one visit, I sang his favourite song—"Shenandoah." When he died in 1994, I learned that one of his last requests was for me to sing that song at his funeral. It was an honour I will never forget. •

Clary Croft and Tom Raddall, Liverpool, 1992.

Donald
MacKay

• • • Nova Scotia has produced some amazing shipbuilders and one of the most famous has to be a Jordan Falls, Shelburne County, man named **Donald MacKay**. He learned the craft as a teen in the local shipyards and took his skills to the United States, where he went on to build some of the largest and most successful clipper ships in the era known as "The Age of Sail." His vessels *Flying Cloud*, *Sovereign of the Seas*, and *Great Republic* ruled the waves. In 1850 *Flying Cloud* set a world's record for speed while taking miners from New York to the newly discovered gold fields of San Francisco in a record eighty-nine days. •

Statue of
Joseph Howe
at Province
House, 2004.

• • • The year 2004 marks the two-hundredth anniversary of the birth of one of Nova Scotia's most illustrious sons. **Joseph Howe** was a printer, newspaperman, politician, poet, and wit. In defending himself in a libel case, he established ground rules for freedom of the press and he played a huge part in bringing responsible government to Nova Scotia. He was premier of Nova Scotia from 1860 to 1863, and although initially against confederation, he later became a member of John A. Macdonald's government in Ottawa. His last public office was that of lieutenant-governor of his beloved province, and he died in office in 1873. A statue of Joseph Howe stands outside Province House. •

• • • In 1797, a Herring Cove orphan and fisherman's apprentice named **Joseph Shortt**, who also went by the nickname Joe Cracker, became a hero when he bravely helped rescue a handful of survivors from the shipwrecked HMS *La Tribune* when it sank near his home. He was hailed for his bravery and visited by Edward the Duke of Kent, who asked the lad what he would like to have as a reward. Joe asked for a pair of trousers and to be able to fish from the beautiful cove he loved. •

• • • *42nd Street* is one of musical theatre's most popular shows, and it was Dartmouth native **Ethel "Ruby" Keeler** who made her movie debut in the 1933 version of the hit show. Born in 1909, Ruby and her family left for the east side of New York when she was three years old. Ms. Keeler became a world-class tap dancer—one of the most famous "hoofers" of the early musical theatre and film era. She was married to the legendary Al Jolsen, and was a well-respected Hollywood luminary and Broadway star. She died in 1993. •

Ruby Keeler, Al Jolsen and Al Jolsen Jr.

• • • The first record of a person of African origin living in Nova Scotia is of a man named Mathieu or **Matthew da Costa**. He is believed to come from the Azores, and it is possible that he was kidnapped by a French merchant, and indentured or enslaved to Pierre duGua, Sieur de Monts. In any event, Mathieu was a crew member of the ship *Jonas* when it left La Rochelle, France, on May 13, 1606, for its voyage to the New World. However, it was not Mathieu's first voyage to these parts. He was well-educated, had been to the area previously in a Portuguese ship, and had learned some of the language of the Mi'kmaq. His services as a translator and experienced voyager were invaluable to the fledgling explorers. He died and was buried at Port-Royal during the winter of 1606-7. •

• • • Pier 21, Halifax's national treasure, has thousands of stories to tell. The majority are of people coming to Canada, but some of the most important stories are of those who helped the newcomers. One such angel of mercy was the multilingual **Sadie Fineberg**, who welcomed people through the gates of Pier 21 for more than forty years, first as the representative of the Jewish Immigration Aid Society, then, starting in 1948, as Halifax's official representative. Whether it was a kind word to feed the spirit or a hamper of food to feed the body, Sadie Fineberg's kindness and largesse are legendary. When she died in 1982 at the age of eighty-two, tributes poured in from all over North America. She was the living, breathing symbol of welcome to Canada! •

Fashion

I have a great interest in the history of fashion. For many years, my wife Sharon and I had a small design business making contemporary one-of-a-kind garments and historic textile and costume reproductions. We're both graduates of the Costume Studies Program at Dalhousie University— Sharon in 1978, I in 1986. Sharon went on to teach the course, and in fact, I missed having my wife as my instructor by one semester. Whew!

Clary Croft in the re-enactment uniform of the Grenadier Company of the 2nd Battalion of His Majesty's 84th Regiment of Foot.

• • • Although it seems ubiquitous today, the distinctive **Nova Scotia tartan** wasn't created until 1953 when it was designed by Bessie Murray. The vivid blue represents the ocean that almost surrounds the province, the white threads represent the surf along the coast, the dark green and the light green represent the evergreen and deciduous trees, the fine gold line represents the Royal Charter granted to Nova Scotia from Scotland in 1621, and the red line represents the lion rampant of the shield found on the flag of Nova Scotia. •

• • • With its vibrant Scottish heritage, it's no wonder New Scotland or Nova Scotia is home to many gentlemen who wear **kilts**. But, heritage aside, there is always one burning question that begs an answer: what is worn under the kilt? I once heard a kilt-wearing friend admonish such a question from a woman by stating, "Madam, it may be old, but it is certainly not worn!" But, for a more accurate reply, *The Modern Tailor, Outfitter and Clothier* (1928) advises its readers that short trews or trousers could be donned if desired. However, most men prefer to wear the kilt military style. You're still curious? A true Scot or Nova Scotian never tells, and a true lady or gentleman never asks! •

• • • **Tattoos** are, once again, back in fashion. That's nothing new in a seafaring province such as ours. The old sailors used jack-knives and sail-needles to pierce their flesh and rubbed in lamp black to make the dark designs. Navy men used tattoos as identification marks: crossed cannons were often worn by a gunner and a fouled anchor by a bosun. I once interviewed a man who worked on sailing vessels, and he told me he and many of his mates believed a tattoo was a form of inoculation and would also prevent them from being drowned. Old salts tattooed a pig on one foot and a rooster on the other; both these creatures despised the water. It was also said that a sailor sporting such a tattoo would never starve. He carried two sources of food—ham and eggs. •

• • • Ask most men to show you the contents of their **wallet** and you'll find some paper money, credit cards, and bits of identification. Not so for the Nova Scotian gentleman of the eighteenth century. Take as example this ad from the *Halifax Gazette*, April 2, 1752: "Lost sometime about the 25th of last month a black leather pocket case lin'd with yellow, with brass clasps, containing some of the Governor's notes and sundry other paper: whoever brings the said case and papers to the subscriber shall have three pounds reward and no questions ask'd." The ad didn't mention that the pocketbook could also contain such items as small diaries, banknotes, hair clippings, knives, tweezers, ear picks and compasses. •

• • • For years, hand-knit **mittens** were an important part of every Nova Scotia fisherman's wardrobe. Worn year-round, the mitts were knit using raw wool, with most of the natural lanolin left in. They were made double the size of the man's hand, shrunk in hot water, then soaked in cold, salted water. The wool would matt, making the mittens almost waterproof. Fishermen said it was bad luck to wear anything but white mittens on a vessel. •

Double pocketbook in Irish stitch; includes sewn-in page inscribed: "Huxford Marchant, His Book, 1772."

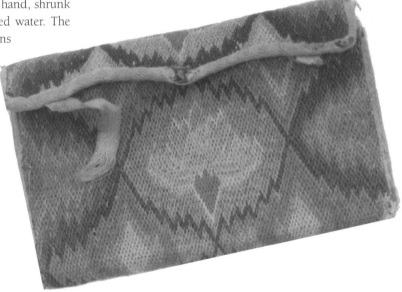

Stanfield's is one of the province's oldest and most-respected clothing manufacturers. The company was founded by Charles E. Stanfield, who emigrated from England to North America in 1855. He began a woolen mill in Prince Edward Island and in 1870 founded the Truro Woolen Mills in that Nova Scotia town. He introduced Canadian men to the concept of heavy ribs in underwear, and more importantly, to the trap or drop seat. Charles eventually passed his strong business sense on to his two sons, John and Frank, who developed the "Shrink-proof Process", underwear that was indispensable during the Klondike Gold Rush of 1898. Contracts to supply long underwear to soldiers in World War I led to recognition for the company across Canada, especially when John, who saw active service in 1915, organized the 193rd Highland Brigade, known affectionately as

Stanfield's Woollens Plant, Truro, NS, 1941.

"Stanfield's Unshrinkables." But, you may ask, are long-johns named after John Stanfield? Not quite. The term long-johns comes from the world of boxing. In the 1880s, John L. Sullivan was a famous fighter—the last bare-fisted champion of the world. He always wore long, underwear-like tights during his fights and they became known as "John L's" or "long-johns." •

Larrigan made in Bridgewater by the Mackenzie Crowe Manufacturing Company

• • • **Larrigans** were a type of leather foot-covering once popular with woodsmen working the forests of Nova Scotia. They were made from leather, frequently cow hide, and tanned and saturated with oil, making them almost waterproof. They were worn over several pairs of woolen socks and were often heelless and smooth on the bottom. Many men made their own, but you could also buy a pair made in Bridgewater by the Mackenzie Crowe Manufacturing Company. If left to dry out, larrigans became hard, wizened, and cracked. A common insult years ago was to say someone looked so old and wrinkled that their face resembled an old larrigan! •

• • • Few of us today ever pause to think where the **colours** for our clothes come from. But years ago, many Nova Scotians had to make their own dyes from natural sources. Alder bark made a black dye, onion skins provided yellow, lichens from rocks and trees gave purples and reds. There were some imported dyes: logwood and indigo—a precursor to the ubiquitous blue denim—gave the common navy blue so popular in everyday clothes. Many of the early dyes were set with urine, and I have read accounts of farmers coming to town in home-dyed homespun jackets that reeked in the hot sun. •

• • • Eighteenth-century Nova Scotia **gentlemen** of quality dressed as lavishly as their European counterparts, and at times, even the working classes rose to a certain level of fashion. After John Robinson and Thomas Rispen traveled about the colony in 1774, they wrote, "The men wear their hair queu'd, and their clothing, except on Sundays, is generally homemade…they dress exceedingly gay on a Sunday, and wear the finest cloth and linen. Many of them wear ruffled shirts…and there is so great a difference in their dress, that you would scarce know them to be the same people." To no lesser degree, the pioneer ladies of early Nova Scotia also made a favorable impression upon John Robinson and Thomas Rispen. About the distaff side they wrote, "The women, in general, (except on Sundays) wear woolseys both for petticoat and aprons…nor on the Sabbath are they any less gay than the men, dressing for the most part in silks and calicoes, with long ruffles; their hair dressed high…when at church or meeting, from mistress to scullion girl, they have all their fans. We ever thought, in the article of dress, they out did the good women of England." •

Costume drawings by Clary Croft based on Robinson & Rispin accounts.

• • • Some of Nova Scotia's early **female** inhabitants could equal and even outshine their contemporaries in London. As an example, take this extract from the letter of a young woman describing the ball dress of Frances Wentworth, wife of the lieutenant-governor: "Mrs. Wentworth stood first in fashion and magnificence. Her gown and petticoat of sylvian tissue trimmed with Italian flowers and the finest blond lace, a train of four yards long, her hair and wrist ornamented with real diamonds." •

Lady Frances Wentworth, by John Singleton Copley

• • • At one time female **nurses** in most clinics, hospitals, and private offices in Nova Scotia were required to wear starched, white caps. (Although, the male nurses never had to wear them.) That, and the amount of time it took to maintain their crisp condition, were two of the main reasons why the white nurses' cap has been relegated to memory. It was a popular move, at least with the nurses. In fact, in 1988, the traditional white cap with black and gold bands was voted out at Dalhousie University's School of Nursing by a referendum—110 against and only 15 people for. •

Medical students studying chest x-rays, Dalhousie University, Halifax, NS, March 4-6, 1947.

• • • **Paisley** patterns reign as some of the most popular motifs in clothing and home decorating. In eighteenth- and nineteenth-century Nova Scotia, it was the paisley shawl that was a must-have clothing accessory for the fashionable. In Halifax and elsewhere in Maritime Canada, shawls were sold to the fashion-minded and became important status symbols of the rising middle class. The *Acadian Recorder* of November 25, 1854, carried an advertisement by Keyran Skerry of Granville Street for "rich filed paisley long shawls." Seven years later, in 1861, the same newspaper stated that "elegant paisley long shawls from 20 shillings to 10 pounds" could be had at the shop of Samuel Strong, Granville Street. •

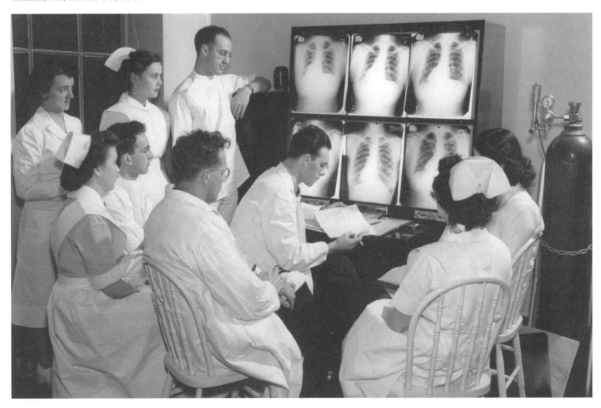

Samuel Vetch, Governor of Nova Scotia 1710-1712 & 1715-1717

• • • In eighteenth-century Nova Scotia, men of authority and social stature wore white or grey **wigs** made from various substances, including human, goat, and horse hair. These wigs required considerable maintenance, and professional wig-makers were often employed to keep them deloused, powdered, and freshly curled. But some fellows, or at least their servants, also did home maintenance—at least when it came to keeping the wigs properly curled. Archeological evidence from eighteenth-century Halifax has produced clay wig-rollers. Fortunately, men didn't have to undergo the discomfort of wearing the curlers to bed. The wigs were dressed off the head, which was usually shaved clean to keep down the lice. •

Flora and Fauna

Nova Scotia has to be one of the most beautiful places on earth. Our natural resources are a precious and treasured thing—at least for most of us. But, all is not perfect in our land. So far, in my lifetime, we see far fewer deer along the roadside and a taste of wild salmon from my birthplace along the St. Mary's River is something I can only remember with sadness. If it is true we learn from our mistakes, we haven't been paying much attention.

Donald Campagna, Clary's father-in-law, with young moose at Shuben-acadie c.1938.

• • • Nova Scotia's official floral emblem is the **mayflower**. It is a fitting symbol; the Nova Scotia Philanthropic Society chose it as its own emblem in 1834 and adopted a fitting motto in reference to the tiny pink and white early spring flowers: "We bloom amid the snow." The 1901 Statutes of Nova Scotia reads, "The trailing arbutus, commonly known as the mayflower, is hereby declared to be, and from time immemorial to have been, the floral emblem of Nova Scotia." Nevertheless, in 1918, the Commonwealth of Massachusetts also adopted the mayflower as its official floral symbol. Now it's the official flower of both places. •

• • • Nova Scotia has its own official provincial dog. It's the Nova Scotia **duck-tolling retriever**. The dogs, which resemble large foxes with their red coats and pointed snouts, used to be bred to toll or lure water fowl by running back and forth to attract them. There are few working tollers today, but they have become popular pets and are not only beautiful dogs, but make great companions. •

• • • **Moose** were once abundant in Nova Scotia's forests. The Mi'kmaq used the hide for clothing which was sewn using moose sinew, and made moose-bone needles, while the long hairs were used for embroidery. The Mi'kmaq believe to dream of moose ensures a long life. Moose calves are born in May and June, and if exposed to human contact, can imprint themselves and become pets. Years ago, young moose were raised in captivity as pets and some were even hitched to sleighs and wagons. •

Marley, the duck-tolling retriever.

• • • The **black bear** is the only member of the ursine family native to Nova Scotia. Ancient people throughout the world linked the bear closely to humans because it is one of the few creatures that walks forward, heel first as we do. The Mi'kmaq called the bear *Mouin*. They tell a tale of a boy who was lost and adopted by a mother bear and her cubs. She taught him the ways of the bear family, including smelt-fishing and hunting. The people eventually saw the boy, captured him, and took him home, where he grew to be the patriarch of the bear clan. •

• • • The government of Nova Scotia once owned a line of provincial studs…We're talking horses here! In 1842, the **Morgan**, one of the most popular breeds of horse, was introduced to Nova Scotia. The government decided to strengthen the Morgan's bloodlines in the province by buying a stallion that they hoped would be the father of many generations of strong yet gentle horses. The stallion's name was Bell Founder Morgan. He began work in 1842 and was retired and sold at auction in 1850. A short career, but no doubt, a pleasant one! •

• • • The poor **crow** has a bad reputation in folklore. Fishermen consider it bad luck for a crow to cross the bow of a boat; you either have to come home and start your journey over, or spit so it won't harm you with bad luck. An Acadian belief from West Pubnico is that a crow standing on the roof of a house is a sign of bad luck. And in several areas of the province, including Guysborough and Lunenburg counties, I have seen exemplified the belief that to keep crows from your garden you must kill one and hang it on the fence. •

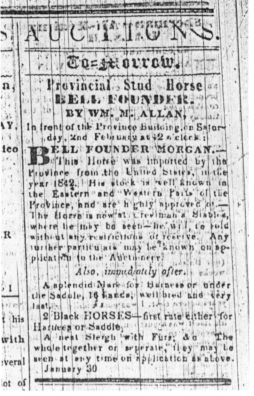

Advertisement for auction of Bell Founder Morgan. *Halifax Sun,* February 1, 1850.

• • • Nova Scotians who own **cats** are proud of their feline friends, but perhaps none more so than those who have polydactyl cats also known as United Empire Loyalist cats. Polydactyl cats are those with six or more toes on their front feet and five or more on the back. Halifax and Yarmouth are among the three or four places in North America with a high percentage of polydactyl cats. In addition to being multi-toed, many of the polydactyl cats in Nova Scotia are calicoes, possessing mottled red, black and cream-coloured fur. Geneticists speculate that these types of cats were deemed special by the early New England colonists and that Loyalists brought them to Nova Scotia after the American Revolution. •

• • • According to eyewitnesses, there just may be a **mystery marsupial** in Nova Scotia. In October 1986, there were sightings at Lochaber, Antigonish County, of a kangaroo-like creature and evidence of three-toed animal prints. A spokesman for the Department of Lands and Forests who went to the area to investigate and photograph the prints is quoted in the Halifax *Daily News* as saying the creatures, "are similar to a kangaroo or wallaby." He could, however, offer no explanation as to what made the prints. Curiously, another man near in the same county claimed he saw a "roo" in the beams of his car's headlights. In January of 1987, the Halifax *Daily News* offered a five-hundred-dollar reward for information about the creature, which by then had also been sighted near the Halifax Airport and at Cole Harbour. To date, no one has been able to claim the money. •

• • • Once pandemic in numbers, brightly painted **wooden butterflies** attached to the sides of houses or barns are still popular in eastern Canada. But why this need to have butterflies attached to one's house? In Scotland there is a folk belief that if you see three butterflies it is bad luck. That's obviously not a belief here in Nova Scotia because many of the butterflies are seen in a trio of graduated sizes on the sides of houses. The butterfly tradition began here as folk art made by people for their own homes, but gradually the insects infiltrated the tourist market. That still doesn't tell us why we nail them to our homes. One explanation I heard is that in Norway it is good luck for a butterfly to land on your house, and the belief was brought to Nova Scotia by Norwegian immigrants. Someone told me it was a Mi' kmaw belief that butterflies bring luck to a camp, and the children would stick them to the sides of the wigwams. My friends in the Mi'kmaw community, however, were not aware of this belief. •

• • • Have you ever wondered why **dalmatian dogs**, with their distinctive black and white markings, are associated with firehouses? It seems dalmations, like goats, get along well with horses and were kept in fire stations to calm the horses that pulled the pumping machinery before motorized trucks took over. It is also said that they ran ahead to clear a path for the horses and calm them so they would rush toward a burning building. They became a part of the firehouse tradition, and even after the introduction of motorized fire engines, the pets remained popular. During the 1950s, all Halifax stations had a dalmatian, donated by the Olands Brewing Company, but the concrete floors proved too hard for the dogs' foot pads, and the animals were retired. •

Dalmation fire dog with firefighter George Branch, at the Bedford Row Fire Station, Halifax, c.1950.

Andrew Downs, 1892

• • • Pity the poor **snake**. He takes a bum rap in many folk beliefs. In Nova Scotia's Shelburne County, snakes were thought of as your enemy—they were to be killed as soon as they appeared in the spring. Another bit of Nova Scotian snake lore states that a snake's colour is the colour of the clothing of your enemy. From Ship Harbour comes the belief that if you kill the first three snakes you ever see you will conquer your enemies for life. At Sherbrooke I was told if you try to kill a snake, it will not die until the sun goes down. And, at Seabright, Helen Creighton collected the belief that dreaming of a snake brought sickness. But please…give the poor creature a break. It is also said that wearing a snake skin around your body can cure aches. Well, I guess either way the snake still ends up dead, so enjoy the ancient lore, but let the snake pass by unharmed. •

• • • Nova Scotia was home to North America's first **zoo**. Andrew Downs, a native of New Jersey, came to Halifax to operate a plumbing business in the 1840s but turned his interest in the study of flora, fauna and taxidermy into a serious pursuit by opening his zoological gardens at Dutch Village, near the North West Arm, in 1847. The zoo featured both live and stuffed birds, Brazilian monkeys, Chinese geese and swans, cranes, beaver, mink, moose, black bear, and even a polar bear. •

• • • **Hemp**, first brought to North America by settlers in the 1600s, is back in favour. Early Acadians grew and harvested hemp. Hemp products were vital to the age of sail: ships used hemp for rope and sails; short hemp fibres were used as oakum, a form of caulking. In 1788, premiums were offered by the Nova Scotian government for the commercial cultivation of hemp, but it didn't seem to have been taken up with any success. Industrial growth was eventually banned in Canada in 1938 because, like marijuana, hemp is a member of the cannabis family. However, hemp's many values are being reinvestigated. Health Canada issued a release in 1998 stating "For the first time in 60 years, Canadian farmers who meet the required provisions can now plan to grow hemp…." The first new crop was planted at Kentville by the Nova Scotia Department of Agriculture. •

Consumers Cordage, Wyse Road, Dartmouth, c.1915. In the 1950s, Dartmouth manufacturers made cordage using manila hemp, which is derived from a type of banana tree.

• • • Some of the **plagues** of the pharaohs were also visited upon Nova Scotians. Early French writers gave accounts of mice and locust plagues in the Maritimes as early as the 1600s. They said these plagues occurred every seven years, but never together. In 1775, there were accounts of mice eating most of the crops in the ground, including the potato crop as it lay in the fields. *The Journal of the Nova Scotia Assembly*, records an 1842 petition from people in Inverness County, Cape Breton, seeking funds to tide them over because mice ate their crops. Allotments were granted from the funds allocated for road maintenance, and those who received this money could work off the debt by performing road work. •

• • • Although they are now gone from Nova Scotia, the woodland **caribou** was native to the province for thousands of years. It was one of the primary food and clothing sources for the Mi'kmaq. However, woodland fires in the late eighteenth and early nineteenth centuries destroyed much of the white reindeer moss that was the principal food source of the caribou, and in the 1890s supply meat ships were reported to be herding caribou off cliffs in northern Cape Breton at a site named Meat Cove. The population dwindled and the last legally shot caribou was taken by J. A. Knight at Cheticamp, Cape Breton, in 1912. By 1921, caribou were considered extinct in Nova Scotia. In 1939, an attempt to reintroduce caribou in the Liscomb Game Reserve proved unsuccessful. In 1964, a study conducted on caribou, moose, and deer confirmed that the deer carried the nematode parasite (roundworm), which attacked the nervous systems of the moose and caribou. However, in 1968 and 1969, another attempt to re-introduce caribou to Nova Scotia saw several animals from Quebec released in northern Cape Breton. It too was unsuccessful. The last confirmed sighting of a caribou in this province was on September 14, 1969, near Ingonish. •

• • • We all know the **folk belief** about killing a spider—you're bound to get rain! Well, here are a few more folk beliefs found in Nova Scotia concerning arachnids:

> **A spider on your clothes means a new item of clothing.**
> **A spider on your hand means a new pair of gloves.**
> **A spider on your foot—a new pair of boots.**
> **See a spider crawl on you and you'll get a new suit of clothes.**

But remember—let the spider live! An old verse advises us:

> **Let a spider run alive; all the days you'll live and thrive. •**

• • • **Walrus** were once common along the shores of Nova Scotia. With the arrival of European adventurers in the 1600s, they began to be hunted for oil and ivory. Nicolas Denys reports that in 1642, four hundred tusks were taken. An old name for walrus was "seacows" and in 1847, Abraham Gesner wrote that the Maritime provinces were once "the resort of great numbers of walrus or seacow.... Hundreds of these animals were killed on the land by the early inhabitants, among whose descendants pieces of their skins still remain in use....Only a few of those noble animals are now seen ...". That was in 1847, but by 1869, when Campbell Hardy wrote an article titled *Forest Life in Acadia*, he stated, "The walrus, once numerous on the coasts, seems to have entirely disappeared." However, occasionally a walrus does stray our way from its more northerly habitat. The last official sighting of a walrus in our waters was that of a juvenile in the waters off Halifax's Point Pleasant Park in 2000. •

Walrus "Trichechidae Rosmanus" by Dr. J.B. Gilpin and lithographed by Clarke's, Halifax, NS. Note reads: "Extinct in Nova Scotia, last seen alive at Sable Island."

Food

I adore food! I like reading about it,
shopping for it, preparing it, and as seen
by my constant battle of the bulge,
eating it. What more can I say?
I loved researching this topic.

• • • Formally established in 1807, the Halifax City **Farmers' Market** holds the distinction of being the oldest continuing institution in Halifax and is one of the oldest markets in Canada. It began in the eighteenth-century at Cheapside and Bedford Row, near the present-day Art Gallery of Nova Scotia. Its location changed several times, settling at the historic Keith's Brewery building on the waterfront. When he visited Halifax, Charles Dickens described the market as "abundantly supplied and exceedingly cheap." Today it's a Halifax institution, and shopping at the market is the best thing anyone can do on a Saturday morning! •

Market Square, corner of Bedford Row and George Street, Halifax, looking northeast from Cheapside, July 1886.

• • • Ah, the joys of a **lobster** dinner! It's one of Nova Scotia's great treats! That wasn't always the case. Years ago children would hide their lobster sandwiches under a rock outside the school so the other kids wouldn't know they were so poor that all they had to eat was lobster. My wife's grandfather, Seymour Brown, told me of growing up in Herring Cove, just outside Halifax, and longing for a baloney sandwich to take to school. He had to settle for lobster. After all it was so plentiful it was free. In fact, lobsters were once so abundant that they could be gathered from among the rocks at low tide. •

• • • **Chewing gum** comes in a myriad of flavours, shapes, and grades of sugar content. Some of it is made especially for diabetics or denture-wearers—the list is endless. But for a real treat, just take a walk in the forest and pick some spruce gum. The natural resin from spruce trees drools out through the bark and forms amber/grey bulblets of pure, sweet flavour. Nova Scotians once harvested this delicious spruce gum and sold it at a hefty profit. The *Halifax Morning Chronicle* of March 21, 1889, carried a notice of three tons of spruce gum being shipped to the United States, worth sixty-eight cents per pound. During the 1940s entire families worked at collecting, sorting, and selling spruce gum, primarily to American markets. However, by the 1950s, sales and interest in this delicious natural treat had waned. But the raw product is still available, and, as they say, there for the picking! •

• • • Nova Scotians enjoy some pretty interesting, and some might say exotic, foods. We even make up **rhymes** about them—
Herrin' and taters, the food of the land,
if you don't like it, you can starve and
be damned.
Antigonish, Antigonish,
boiled potatoes and salty fish. •

• • • If rhyming doesn't move you, perhaps a unique nomenclature will. Take for instance the term **Digby chicks**. Folk history tells us that the first eighteenth-century settlers arrived at Digby during the autumn, but before they could get settled, winter set in. When Christmas came there were no fowl for the traditional dinner; in fact there was no fresh meat at all, only salt and smoked fish. So, the people called their smoked herring "Digby chicken" and served it up for their Christmas fare. •

Two fishermen with a tuna,
Herring Cove, c.1958.

• • • Nova Scotia was once the **tuna-fishing** capital of the world. In the eighteenth- and nine-teenth-centuries, English-speaking fishermen called tuna "albacore," "sea lions," or "horse mackerel," while their Acadian counterparts knew the giants as "gros pêche." But Nova Scotians rarely ate tuna until around 1903 when the immigrant Italian population of Boston started the demand for the fish they knew at home. We shipped it down to the Boston States, then developed a taste for tuna ourselves, even though one local recipe called for the flesh to be boiled for half an hour then pan fried like a pork steak. It's now offered as fresh steaks in posh restaurants and marketed to the Japanese for sushi and sashimi—a far cry from boiled and fried "horse mackerel." •

• • • When the large wave of **German settlers** began arriving in Halifax in 1750, moving to Lunenburg in 1752, they brought and shared much of their food from the mother country. Many of those foods still retain remnants of their original names. People of German heritage in this province are often called "Dutch" (from the German *Deutsch*), so a dish of salt cod, pork scraps, onions and potatoes is still called "house-banking" or "Dutch mess." "Kartoffel" or "kuduffle," from the German *die kartoffel* for potato, is soup made with noodles, potatoes, and a gravy made from browned flour. "Snits," from the German *schnitten*—to cut—are dried apple slices. And, *handkäse* and *krishelo* are words used to describe a type of hand-made cheese made of curds, cream, nutmeg or caraway seeds and butter and formed into cakes. •

• • • *L'Ordre de Bon Temps*, or the **Order of Good Cheer**, is North America's oldest social club. It was conceived and named by Samuel de Champlain, who helped established Port-Royal in Nova Scotia in 1605. In part, the celebrations helped the colonists through the long, harsh winters. Part of the celebrations involved elaborate feasts. A typical menu would consist of duck, grey and white geese, partridge, lark, moose, caribou, beaver, otter, rabbit, fat beaver's tail, wildcat, raccoon and sturgeon, accompanied by fruit, vegetables, bread, pastries and wine. •

• • • **Spruce beer** was once a very common drink for many Nova Scotians. In the eighteenth century, during the occupation of Louisbourg, the British manufactured and drank spruce beer because they thought the water was contaminated. (At least that was their excuse!) Twice a week, ten soldiers from each brigade were delegated to gather the spruce boughs and make the beer. Tender strips of spruce were boiled for three hours, the liquid strained into a wooden cask, and molasses added. The British used a ratio of six quarts of molasses to a barrel of water, while the French used four quarts—they preferred a drier beverage! •

• • • Nova Scotia **smoked salmon** is world famous. Just ask any New Yorker what you need for the quintessential lox and bagel. The man who made his, and our, reputation in the smoked salmon trade was Willy Krauch, whose family still operates the business he began in 1956 in the beautiful village of Tangier. Buckingham Palace has a standing order for Willy's famous delicacy and it's equally at home at a Northumberland Shore picnic. But here's a little secret we need to keep under our hats: Willy's Nova Scotia method for smoking salmon is actually a version of one he brought from his native Denmark. Perhaps we should be saluting both nations for this superb treat. Regardless of its origin, we are indebted to Willy; he's made smoked salmon our own and we salute him for it. •

• • • Residents of, and visitors to, Nova Scotia's capital city are offered an overwhelming variety of places to dine. It seems this was always the case. Halifax was founded in 1749, and twenty years later, there were upwards of one hundred licensed houses in the town, the most famous being the **Great Pontack Inn**, operated by John Willis. An ad in the *Halifax Gazette* informed Willis' patrons that "the proprietor also proposes to keep a chophouse, where gentlemen may be supplied with the greatest dispatch…and [can be served] hot mutton pies every day." And, while you waited for your hot pie, they would also arrange to have your market cattle slaughtered at the nearby slaughterhouse. I don't think anyone offers the same service today! •

• • • Here's a **folk riddle** from Oakland, Nova Scotia:
A little white house all filled with meat,
no windows or doors to get in to eat.
What is it?
It's an egg, also known to some Nova Scotians by its folk name—"hen's fruit." But "eggs" didn't always mean chicken eggs. In the Chezzetcook area people used to go "egging." They would row to the out-islands and gather gull, wild duck, and pigeon eggs. In the nineteenth century, these eggs found eager buyers each weekend at the Halifax Farmers' Market. Eggs also played an important part in the folk beliefs found in Nova Scotia. An old cure for tuberculosis from Paddy's Head was to eat a white egg laid by a black hen. At Glen Haven, folklore collector Helen Creighton was told that a tiny egg was unlucky—throwing it over the roof of the house would bring back the luck. And in several localities in the province, Dr. Creighton was told that eggs without yolks are known as "witch eggs." If a hen lays such an egg, she must be a witch's familiar—to destroy the familiar, the hen had to be buried alive. •

• • • If you're like me and like most Nova Scotians, you have a real sweet tooth. We love all kinds of **baked goods**—from pies and cakes to cookies and squares. Many non-Maritimers are unfamiliar with the term "square"—those little cake-like bars that are so popular at bridal showers and social teas. In other places, they are more commonly called bar cookies. It's all in the name! In Shelburne county they call cupcakes dory plugs, and gingerbread is not really a bread; it's eaten for dessert or as breakfast fare. Some people insist that a Washington pie, which is a cake layered with jam or cream, be left plain on top, while others smother it in chocolate. Some desserts have several folk names, depending upon the occasion and company in which they are served. Several years ago I was introduced to a sticky, gooey chocolate dessert the hostess called "Sex in a Pan." It was that good! Teaching a folklore class to a group of visitors from the United States a few years later, I talked about this folk name. I was informed that they had the same dessert, except when they took it to church socials it was toted as "Ecstasy in a Pan." •

• • • Historians believe **apples** were first planted in Nova Scotia at Port-Royal in 1606. The early French settlers brought a long tradition of apple cultivation from their farms in Normandy. In fact, in 1699, a French writer named Villebon said that "Port Royal is a little Normandy for apples." However, he also reported the settlers were neglecting the apple crop and the harvests were not as good as he felt they could be. That certainly changed with the times. New England Planters worked hard to develop the apple industry, and from the mid-eighteenth century until 1849 Nova Scotia saw a dramatic rise in local production and consumption. And it was in 1849 that Nova Scotians began exporting apples to Great Britain—a tradition that is still carried on today. Even now, the bulk of our Macintosh crop is sent abroad, and I have purchased apples in a market in Grenoble, France, labelled simply "Canadas." I probably travelled halfway 'round the world to eat an apple grown at home. •

• • • **Salt** has been harvested in Nova Scotia for millennia. The Mi'kmaq used salt springs and evaporated salt from tidal pools. Salt was a major trade commodity from the West Indies and was vital to our manufacture of salt fish, so naturally, it was to our advantage to find a cheap local source. It is believed that early salt extraction in Nova Scotia was by the brine method—pouring hot water down a shaft and evaporating the extracted liquid. Rock salt, however, is mined in its hard state from underground shafts or pits. But before 1900 there were no rock salt mines in Canada. That all changed when a farmer, Peter Murray, was digging a well near the Northumberland Shore to provide water for his cattle and he came up with salt water. Relatively soon after, at Malagash on September 2, 1918, the first rock salt was mined in Canada. By 1954 the Canadian Salt Company discovered huge salt deposits at Pugwash, which is still a major source for salt in Canada today. •

Salt mines at Pugwash, 1961

• • • Whether as food source or popular Halloween icon, **pumpkins** are familiar to Nova Scotians. The folklore surrounding these members of the gourd family is rich and varied, but no aspect of pumpkin life is so interesting as the Halloween jack-o-lantern. In many Celtic cultures, jack-o-lanterns were hollowed-out turnips or large potatoes, filled with fire to ward off evil spirits on the most scary of nights—All Hallow's Eve. When our Celtic ancestors came to the New World, they found giant pumpkins to make even larger lanterns, and the symbolism has remained to this day. But we have even better pumpkin bragging rights here: Nova Scotia's pumpkin potentate Howard Dill began growing giant pumpkins in the 1960s, producing a world champion in 1976. •

Spa Springs, Wilmot, Nova Scotia, circa 1890.

Nova Scotia's pumpkin potentate Howard Dill.

• • • Natural **spring waters** and bottled water, now commonplace worldwide, are certainly not a new phenomena to Nova Scotians. In the nineteenth century, Spa Springs in the Annapolis Valley became famous for its water. The Mi'kmaq used the wet mud from the spring to cure skin wounds; by the 1820s, European settlers were familiar with the spring's properties, and the public flocked to the healing mud and its waters. Spa Springs' first hotel was built in 1832 and guests included Samuel Cunard, Joseph Howe, and Alexander Keith. The effects of the waters at the spa caused many people to publish testimonials in the provincial papers. A brochure from the 1860s boasted: "It is a delicious, healthful beverage, it quenches the thirst. Prevents fermentation, aids digestion…cures indigestion and sick headaches…as a medicinal water it is useful in Bright's disease, disease of the kidneys, diabetes, and disease of the urinary organs, fever, skin diseases, rheumatism, gout, liver complaint, dyspepsia, etc., etc." •

• • • Even though we are almost surrounded by the sea, Nova Scotians have a long tradition of **meat** consumption. The early Acadians salted mutton and pork for use during the long winters, and they frequently gave cattle, hogs, and sheep as wedding gifts. German settlers sold their veal, mutton, and pork sausages to the thriving markets in Halifax. Food purveyors in Halifax coffee houses sold hot mutton pies, beef soup, and mutton broth. Our ancestors had many beliefs about the preparation of these foods. In days gone by, people butchered pork and beef with the full moon so the meat would not shrink. The famous Lunenburg puddings are actually sausages made with fresh pork and spices. And according to some folks in Lunenburg County, sausage eaten with sauerkraut will not "repeat on you." •

• • • In 1728, Scotland forbade the growing of **potatoes** because they were not mentioned in the Bible. The ban wasn't much of a success, still the ideology persisted into the nineteenth century. As late as 1857, an editorial in the *Presbyterian Witness* (Nova Scotia) stated:

It is, we believe, now generally admitted that the failure in the potato crop is to be traced to the direct interference of the Almighty and is to be regarded as a punishment inflicted upon man for his presumption in attempting to introduce disorder into the economy of nature by giving an undue prominence to the potato, to the supplanting of other production of the vegetable kingdom.

However, not many Nova Scotians held this belief. Folks of Scottish heritage enjoyed tatties and neeps, Lunenburgers ate a potato soup called *kartofelsuppe*, and in Halifax the Irish settlers had corned beef and Irish cobbler. And since 1977, Haligonians have been enjoying hand-cut fries from the chip wagon of "Bud the Spud". •

Bud the Spud, Spring Garden Road, Halifax, 2004.

• • • Food shopping in Halifax has certainly seen dramatic changes in the past sixty years. **Grocery stores** began to make major changes in the 1940s. The Acadian Stores, located at the corner of Windsor and Almon streets, opened a new style of store in May of 1948. The *Halifax Mail* noted that it was a self-service store—people actually helped themselves from shelves and display cases instead of having clerks fill their orders from produce behind a counter. Frank's Automat, Halifax's first automat, opened in 1962, operating for a brief time on Blowers Street. •

• • • **Scallops** are considered a great seafood delicacy and Digby scallops are world-renowned for their size and flavour. The scallop fishery in Digby dates to about the 1920s, and Digby's first shipment to the Boston market was in 1925. One of the best areas for fishing scallops was, and continues to be, the George's Banks, between Nova Scotia and New England. According to William Hamilton in his book *The Nova Scotia Traveller*, the best beds on the George's Banks were located by rum-runners. Forced by bad weather and United States Coast Guard surveillance to spend many idle hours on the Banks, the rum-runners soon discovered a more legitimate way of getting rich. •

• • • Nova Scotia's favorite traditional **spirit**—strong drink—has always been black rum. To say rum was a popular drink in early Nova Scotia would be a gross understatement. In a letter written in May of 1760, Halifax councillor Alex Grant complained to the Reverend Ezra Stiles in Boston, "The business of one-half of the town is to sell rum, and the other half to drink it." Many folk names have evolved to describe this delicious nectar from the sugar cane. Old sailors used to call it rusty water. You may still hear someone say they spent the night partying with the captain—Captain Morgan that is. But my favorite folk expression for rum comes from the land of the *Bluenose*, where good black rum is known as Lunenburg champagne. •

• • • The Truro Condensed Milk and Canning Company was the first dairy in Canada to produce **condensed milk**. First manufactured under the Reindeer brand in 1883, the milk won prizes at European food fairs. In a lengthy advertisement, the *Truro Guardian* of 1883 announced that the Truro Condensed Milk and Canning Factory opened in June and was started by Charles Graham of Halifax, who saw similar factories in the New England states. He chose Truro because of the good access to shipping and the excellent sources for cheap coal to fire the evaporators. It didn't hurt that labour costs in Canada were fifteen to twenty percent lower than in the American markets. The factory used ten tons of milk a day to make six thousand cans of evaporated milk. •

• • • **Tea** continues to be a very popular Maritime Canadian drink. In fact, aside from water, tea is the world's most popular drink, and Maritimers consume twenty-five percent of the tea in Canada. It's so common today we take it for granted, but years ago, it was an expensive and highly-prized commodity. It's believed that the first tea shipment to come directly from China to Halifax was landed from the vessel *Countess of Harcourt* in 1826. It brought 6,517 chests of fine china tea. The rage for coffee and the fun of rolling up the rim came later! •

• • • If you're like me, you love getting **chocolate** for Christmas (or any day of the year for that matter.) For many years, Nova Scotians have enjoyed a special brand of this confection from the famous Moirs Chocolate Company. The firm was established as the Moir and Company Steam Bakery and Flour Mill. They began making chocolate in 1873. However, their most famous confection, the Pot of Gold assortment of boxed chocolates, wasn't conceived until the 1920s, when it became an instant hit. In peak production years, Moirs could turn out more than two million boxes of Pot of Gold. I fondly remember the days when the Moirs factory stood on the site of the present World Trade and Convention Centre in Halifax. The smells alone coming out of that place were enough to satisfy a chocoholic for days! •

• • • Our eighteenth-century ancestors might not have had the mega-grocery stores we have today, but many of them fared quite well. As an example, take this list of items sold at Edward deWolf's **general store** at Horton Landing, Nova Scotia, from December 1793 to July of 1794: "Allspice, annis [sic], butter, cake, cider, clove water, cloves, cod, coffee, cordials, corn, flour, hops, molasses, mustard, mutton, nutmeg, pepper, raisins, rice, rum, saltpeter, sugar, [three kinds of tea, including a green tea], wheat and wine." Sounds good, doesn't it? •

Halifax Harbour showing
the Moirs' Factory tower.

TOWN CLOCK AND HARBOR, HALIFAX, N. S.

Fun and Games

We're a fun-loving bunch here in Nova Scotia. We enjoy sports, making music, and lively games of cards and other games of chance. Visitors are almost always offered a "cup o' tea" or something stronger, and every party congregates in the kitchen. Parties are often more serendipitous than planned. We seem to be easily amused— I always say I'd go to a dog fight if they served a lunch!

• • • At eighteenth-century Louisbourg, lotteries and **gambling** were common and popular with the majority of the population. And, according to court papers for the year 1736, one minor wager turned into a serious situation when it ended up in court. Marie Catherine Auge was expecting a child and Jean Darraq made her a wager that the child would be a boy. If he was wrong, he promised to buy her a new pair of shoes. Darraq went to sea and Marie Catherine delivered a girl. Since she had won the bet, she went to the local cobbler and had a new pair of shoes made, telling the shoemaker to send the bill to Monsieur Darraq. When Monsieur Darraq did not settle his account, the shoemaker took him to court, where he was forced to pay for Marie Catherine's shoes and the additional court costs. The moral, as true today as it was in eighteenth-century Louisbourg: if you make a bet, pay up, or it will cost you more in the end! •

• • • Dartmouth can lay claim to being the home of the first spring-action **skate** to fit over an existing boot. The ACME Skate was invented by John Forbes for the Starr Manufacturing Company. The new patented skate was advertised in 1890 as having "no key, no screws or nuts, no lost parts, requires no previous fitting, always ready to put on." The manufacturers won a gold medal at the Philadelphia Centennial Exposition in 1876 and another at the 1893 Chicago World's Fair. The peak year for ACME Skate manufacturing was 1873. The company had 250 employees and made a profit of 25,000 dollars. They celebrated this event by presenting Lady Dufferin, wife of the governor general, with a pair of gold-plated Starr skates. The 1875 *Encyclopedia Britannica* described the Forbes ACME Skate as the best skate on the market. •

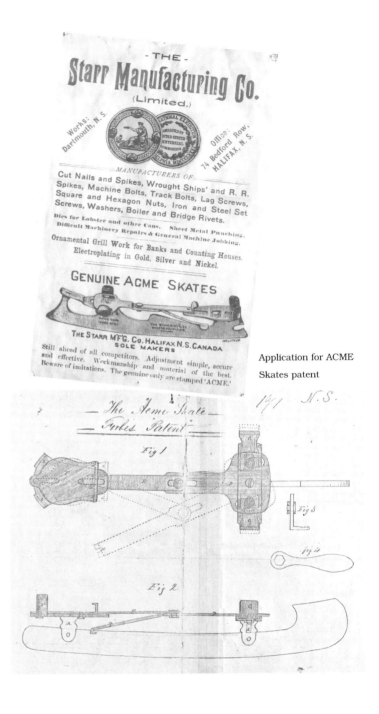

Application for ACME

Skates patent

• • • Nova Scotians and visitors alike enjoy some of the best seaside resorts in the world, and it seems we always did. In the early nineteenth century, visitors could stay at hotels and inns on Halifax's Bedford Basin, where they could dance at lighted pavilions and spear lobsters by torchlight. Spectacular beaches near Halifax also drew huge crowds. In 1895 residents in and around the capital city were enticed to the **seaside** by advertisements such as this:

Why not! Enjoy a day's pleasure,
where you can drive to Cow Bay and
Return for 75 cents.

Isneror's A1 Team leaves his stables,
head of Dartmouth Steamboat Landing
at 10:30 am every Tuesday and Thursday
during the season.
He will welcome and accommodate any
pleasure parties to any number.
A team also leaves for Lawrencetown,
Seaforth and Chezzetcook. •

A picnic at Silver Sands, Cow Bay, Nova Scotia.

Amherst Golf
and Country
Club

• • • Nova Scotians are avid **golfers**, and so it should be! We boast some of the most spectacular courses in Canada—and some of the oldest. The Ashburn Golf Club in Halifax was established as early as 1894. The Amherst Golf and Country Club began on a farm near that town in 1909. The grounds were tended by a local farmer with his plough horse and hay-mower. Membership was ten dollars for men, five dollars for women. Try asking for those rates today when you play the Cape Breton Highland Links course, which, by the way, is considered one of the top twenty courses in the world for beauty. It's true—beauty does have its price! •

• • • **Board games** can be great fun, and it seems Nova Scotians not only enjoy playing them, they enjoy inventing them. Halifax entrepreneur Frank Phillipo developed a game called *Biblical Quest*, with a board shaped like the Star of David. In 1987 Ruth Mersereau and Peter Stucki of Amherst brought out a board game called Rubies and Pearls, which was sold in high-priced jewelry stores. In 1985, sisters Marion and Joy LeBlanc introduced Soapbox, Nova Scotia's first trivia game based on the wildly popular television soap operas. And Atlantic Trivia, created by Larry and Susan Woodman, was introduced in 1984. I found this game particularly interesting, especially for one question: "What musical group represented Canada at the Osaka World's Fair in 1970?" I knew the answer! The Privateers. I was a member of that singing group, and, as a result, am part of the answer to a trivia game. Ah, the dizzying heights of celebrity! •

The Choir of St. Paul's Anglican Church, Halifax, NS, c.1865.

• • • Music has long played an important part of the social lives of people throughout the province. In Lunenburg, a harmonic society was formed in 1828 to promote the singing of sacred music. Twenty-four men joined as charter members—apparently choral singing was not considered proper for women, who were allowed only as visitors. Antigonish had a musical society as early as 1844; Pictou records a philharmonic society giving a series of concerts in 1856 and 1857. In Barrington, a harmonic society was formed in 1861 and lasted well into the 1870s. And by the 1880s and into the 1890s, glee clubs and singing groups associated with temperance societies were abundant. •

• • • Nova Scotia once had a plethora of **singing clubs**, many akin to social glee clubs. In Halifax, the New Union Singing Society was formed in 1809 and the St. Paul's Singing Society was formed in 1819. In 1836 the Amateur Glee Club was organized by young tradesmen and mechanics of Halifax. This group, according to a newspaper account, "afforded pleasure to their friends and innocent amusement to themselves." They gave their first concert, which lasted for three hours and was attended by two hundred people, in May of 1837. While some scoffed, the popular press lauded the musical attempts. *The Novascotian* wrote, "Perhaps some may be disposed to smile at the idea of those who have to live by the labor of their hands, attempting to cultivate a taste for music, or seeking the refining influences of such an association. We are glad, however, to see such a spirit springing up—such a desire manifested to bring within the reach of the middling classes rational pleasures, which are too often believed to belong only to the rich." •

• • • In mid- to late-nineteenth-century Nova Scotia, one of the most popular pastimes for young and old was to gather around the parlor organ and sing hymns and other songs. These **pump organs** were the first popular mass-produced instruments in the nineteenth century. But not everyone was pleased with the new musical innovation. Before there was an organ in the Presbyterian church in my hometown of Sherbrooke, the hymns were started by a presenter, a man who established the pitch with a pitch-pipe or began the singing before the congregation joined in. When the church moved with the times and got an organ, one elderly lady reportedly stood up in her pew and sharply demanded that the "instrument of the devil" be taken out of the church. •

• • • Most Canadians know that **basketball** was conceived by Dr. James Naismith in December 1881, at Springfield, Massachusetts. Dr. Naismith introduced the game to eighteen men, all aspiring YMCA secretaries—and three of those fellows were originally from Nova Scotia. Nova Scotia native Lyman Archibald may have been the first man to bring the game back to Nova Scotia but Finley Macdonald from Pictou and John Thompson from New Glasgow also had an influence on the development of the game. Subsequently, men's basketball was played as early as 1894 at the Halifax YMCA. It was also a sport open to women—a team of girls from the Halifax Academy defeated a boys' team in 1918. •

Basketball team, Edgehill School for Girls, Windsor, NS, 1916.

YMCA Basketball team, 1900.

• • • The **waltz** was the dirty dancing craze of the Victorian era. Britain's *London Times* once called the dance a "voluptuous intertwining of limbs, and close compression of the bodies," and warned its readers, "So long as this obscene display was confined to prostitutes and adulteresses we did not think it deserving of notice; but…we feel it a duty to warn every parent against exposing his daughter to so fatal a contagion." As you can well imagine, such warning only made the dance more popular. But before you judge the naysayers on the other side of the pond too harshly, take a look at how some folks in this province viewed such dancing in 1922. That year, on September 22, the council of Sydney, Cape Breton, debated the morals of allowing dancing in the dark, or what they termed "moonlight waltzes." Apparently, an alderman named Mackenzie was upset one evening when he saw a crowd of young people assembled on a sidewalk on Charlotte Street looking up at a building.

There, behind window blinds, were the silhouettes of couples dancing together. He complained, "A man does not need to be much of a moral crank to see the evil which is engendered by an assemblage such as I have spoken of." •

• • • Stroll the streets of downtown Halifax and you'll find many interesting and quaint **names** attached to the bars, pubs, and restaurants. In earlier times, the same held true. *The Red Cow Inn* was a popular stopping-point for farmers bringing their cattle to market in town. It was situated at the corner of Chebucto and Mumford roads. *The Stag* or *Deer Inn* was operated by William Stag near Preston, while *The Blue Bell Tavern*, on the old highway leading from Halifax to Windsor, is the reason we have Bell Road. •

"Automatic Pin-Setters for Conn-Martell Alleys" *Halifax Chronicle-Herald*, August 15, 1958.

• • • When it opened for business in 1958, the Bayers Road Shopping Centre **Bowlarama** was being advertised in the Halifax papers as a "new bowling academy" with automatic pin-setting facilities. That's a far cry from the earlier days when the pins had to be hand set by pin boys. My father-in-law, Don Campagna, used to work as a pin-boy at Conn and Martel's Bowling Alley on Argyle Street in Halifax during the 1930s. His wages were paid by the bowler—from three to five cents a string. He sat on a bench above the pins and set them in place by hand after each frame was bowled. He said he frequently got hit on the shins by bowlers, who used both the small and large size balls and a range of different style pins. Interestingly, only men bowled. Don said he never saw a female bowler. •

Advertisement to win a radio. *Halifax Mail*, July 2, 1935.

• • • **Radio** continues to be a popular medium in this rapidly changing communications age. You probably enjoy listening to radio from a modern, high-tech receiver in your car, at home or work, or perhaps on a headset as you're moving about. I see dozens of people every day walking about with headsets or earphones attached to portable players and radios. But did you know that all early radios had earphones? In a 1965 article for the *Chronicle Herald,* writer Edith Mosher recalled one man referring to listening in on the earphones as "putting on the ear cups." Early radios had more noise and static than discernable sound. Twenty minutes of programming was considered good quality. On June 25, 1922, the first of a series of test broadcasts was sent out from the Phinneys Music Store building in Halifax from radio station CFCE. The listening public was asked to let the broadcasters know how their signals were being received. In the 1930s and 1940s, in order to listen in, you had to buy a radio licence costing about one dollar a year. Now there's a switch—today you can listen to radio broadcasts for free! •

• • • The first and perhaps most unlucky **tennis** match played in Canada took place in Nova Scotia. Lord William Campbell, the new governor of Nova Scotia in 1766, and Major Milward of the 59th Regiment took on Lord Campbell's new secretary, Captain William Owen, and a Captain Williams at Louisbourg in what is believed to be the first tennis match in the country. But why the unlucky outcome? Captain Owen was accidentally struck on the left eye by his partner's racket and was blinded. •

South End Tennis Club, Halifax, c.1900.

• • • To say fishermen never brag is to admit that fish have feathers. This story comes from the folklore collection of Arthur Huff Fauset, who conducted his research in the province in 1925. John Meyers, a taxi driver from Dartmouth, told Fauset this tale of a renowned fisherman named Crawford from Musquodoboit River. One day Mr. Crawford got together in Power's Barroom with four or five salmon fishermen from Halifax. They were having a few drinks, and an argument arose about **fishing**. One of the men bragged he had caught a fish that weighed forty pounds. Doubting the man's credibility, his companions decided to let Mr. Crawford decide if such a boast could hold true, and they asked him about the biggest fish he ever caught. Mr. Crawford told them he was twenty-five years old when he caught his biggest. "When I pulled it out of the water," he said, "the river fell by two feet." •

Clarence Croft salmon fishing on St. Mary's River, 1992.

• • • Nova Scotians love **card games**. In Cape Breton the game of Tarabish has for some folks reached almost cult status. But it seems the most popular card game in the province is forty-fives, with cribbage coming in a close second (my apologies to the bridge players). And, if you're having bad luck at cards, get up from your chair and walk around it three times. I'm not too sure about this one. I have the worst luck in cards and all this belief ever got me was a trip around the chair. •

• • • I live near Halifax's lovely Public Gardens so I have constant reminders of the damage this spot sustained from hurricane Juan in September 2003. But I am confident that, phoenix-like, the gardens will rise again to its former glory. After all, it has seen many changes over the years. For instance, the Public Gardens was home to the first covered **skating rink** in Canada. Erected by the military in 1859 and measuring sixty by eighty feet, the rink stood on the South Park Street side of the gardens, midway between Sackville Street and Spring Garden Road. During the winter, skating carnivals were held there. The rink was demolished in 1889 to make way for a large building that would house offices, a canteen and washrooms. In 1876, the first public lawn tennis court in Canada was opened in the Gardens on the present site of the children's playground. When I first moved to Halifax in 1955, the gardens boasted a small zoo, featuring monkeys and peacocks. They were removed in the early 1960s. •

• • • The first **play** written and performed in what would become Nova Scotia was a playlet titled *Théâtre de Neptune* (Neptune's Theatre). In fact, it was probably the first play written and performed in any of the French and English colonies. It was penned in 1606 by Marc Lescarbot, a Paris lawyer, poet, and playwright who lived in Acadia from 1606 until 1607. It featured a trident-carrying King Neptune welcoming the comrades back to the New World. To honour this event, Halifax's leading playhouse adopted the name Neptune Theatre. •

• • • Halifax may have a reputation today as a party town, but for many years you had to be a man if you wanted an invitation to the party. **Women** were a mainstay in the grog shops and rum houses of the nineteenth century—women of a certain character, as the early preachers would say—but for most of the twentieth century, women were not allowed to enter a bar and have a drink. A big change came about in 1964 when women were permitted into specially designated-beverage rooms, although initially, they were required to have a male escort. •

Getting Around

I've glided in a gondola in Venice, streaked along in a bullet train in Japan, and gasped at the azure Caribbean from a plane. But for sheer enjoyment, a walk along Nova Scotia's ocean shore or through a woodland park is about as good as it gets. For my money, the best mode of transportation is still "shank's mare"!

• • • Public transport in Halifax began in the earliest days of settlement with **sedan chairs**. These were basically a box with a seat and curtained windows supported by two poles and carried about by two men. Such a conveyance was almost exclusively for the wealthy. Hackney horse cabs and larger horse-drawn conveyances known as omnibuses were popular in the early nineteenth century. In 1866, Halifax introduced a horse-drawn street railway that ran from the train station at Richmond to the south end of the town. Incensed, cab drivers threatened to sabotage the tram line. •

Manager James Adams and most of the conductors, drivers, etc., with two open (summer) horse cars, Halifax Street Railway Co., Halifax, N.S., in front of the company's car barn, S.E. corner of Campbell's Road & Hanover St., Richmond, Halifax, N.S., c.1894

• • • An **automobile** appeared in Halifax as early as 1899, naturally attracting a large crowd. Although that car was an import, Nova Scotia may be the first place in Canada to manufacture automobiles. An announcement in the *Halifax Morning Chronicle* of May 6, 1901, reads: "W.B. Bowser of Amherst will have his horseless carriage ready on May 24…[It is] specially designed for Nova Scotia's rough roads." Ten years later, in 1911, Halifax had 125 registered automobiles—the rest of the province another 485. •

Reg Prescott and car, one of the first in Dartmouth, about 1915.

• • • In 1909, Dartmouth's town council denounced the **recklessness** of certain automobile drivers. One of the primary complaints was that cars were frightening the horses with which they shared the roads. Since the farmers used the roads to make a living, the following bylaw was introduced: "No automobile shall be allowed to run on any road in the municipality of the County of Halifax, except on Tuesday and Thursday each week." The penalty was a fine of fifty to one hundred dollars. A few weeks later a Dartmouth paper prophetically wrote, "The auto has come to stay....In time [it] will be as common as carriages are today...." •

• • • According to the *Guinness Book of Records*, Halifax has a traffic control feature unique in the world. It's found at the corner of Robie Street and Veterans' Way, at the northwest corner of Camp Hill Cemetery. Just inside that fence on that corner is a post that carries a working stop light. It is the only known place in the world where a **stop light** is found in a cemetery. •

Clary Croft beside traffic signal lights in Camp Hill Cemetery, Halifax, 2004.

• • • One of the most recognizable maritime symbols in Nova Scotia is the dory. But the **dory** was once much more than a quaint image on a poster. The strength built into a dory could literally mean life or death to men fishing out on the Grand Banks. The "knees," the dory's rib-like supports, were made from hackmatack or juniper—hard wood to withstand the North Atlantic. The body of the dory was made from pine, and the most common colour for these flat-bottomed boats was yellow, presumably so one could be found in the fog. The dory was the work horse of the schooner, usually manned by two fellows who became dory-mates and learned to work as a team. And even when they weren't fishing, dory-mates would test their skills at dory-rowing and racing. Those skills are still evident today at the International Dory Races, held each year during the Fishermen's Picnic and reunion (part of the Lunenburg Fisheries Exhibition.) •

• • • It is reputed that Halifax has more **taxis** per capita than any city in Canada. Perhaps Halifax's first taxi or hired cab was operated by Richard Holmes, who placed an ad in the *Halifax Gazette* in 1773 advising that his hackney coach was available for hire with driver. While the province's first motor taxi service was organized by G.W. Robinson sometime around 1900, some historians believe that the first auto taxi in Halifax was introduced by Fred Parsons and James Wood in 1911, and they had to coax people into the vehicle. Perhaps this was the beginning of the long-running belief that some taxi drivers are out to fleece the public. Take as example a letter of complaint written to the Halifax *Acadian Recorder* in 1857: "The way Halifax…coachmen impose upon strangers by charging them from four to eight dollars for the use of a miserable rattletrap…is a disgrace to the city…." But lest we tar all miscreants with the same brush, let me say that most of Halifax's cabdrivers are pretty straight shooters. •

Richard "Dickie" Naugle and Gerald Dempsey, c.1955. This team from Herring Cove were champion racers in 1953, 1957 and 1958.

Miss Ada McNab, 1st Lock, Dartmouth Lakes, c.1925.

• • • For millennia, the Mi'kmaq used a water passage consisting of the Shubenacadie River and several connecting lakes to gain access from what is now Dartmouth to the Bay of Fundy near Maitland. A **canal** was suggested by Sir John Wentworth in the eighteenth century, but was not begun until 1826 with the development of the Shubenacadie Canal Company. A series of locks was built, and the canal could have been a success if not for a new mode of transportation. By the time the canal system opened in 1861, it was already considered obsolete by many. A rail line had opened in 1858. •

• • • We tend to think of **stage coaches** as props from the movies. Not so for nineteenth-century Nova Scotians. The 1820 *Nova Scotia Almanac* carried a notice for mail coaches between Halifax and Pictou leaving every Wednesday at one o'clock and arriving at Pictou on Friday—twelve dollars for the one-way passage. The use of public stage coaches in Nova Scotia seems to have ended in 1921. The last ones mentioned in *Belchers Almanac* travelled from Halifax to Sheet Harbour on the eastern shore, and from Halifax to Mahone Bay on the south shore. Neither of these stage runs was listed in 1922. •

Lindsay & Company's Royal Mail Stage Coach ready to start from Lindsay's Stage Office at Antigonish for New Glasgow, NS, probably before 1870.

Ferry *Dartmouth*

Samuel Cunard from a lithograph by W. H. Dickinson.

• • • On February 3, 1752, John Connor was given exclusive rights to operate a **ferry** service between Halifax and Dartmouth, inaugurating a tradition that continues today—the oldest saltwater ferry service in the world. While today's commuters can mingle and enjoy the trip from either below or above deck, in years gone by and up until 1956, when the new passenger-only ferries came into commission, the inside sitting areas were segregated: men occupied one side of the ferry, while women and children held sway in the other. At least that's what the signs said: this rule was rarely, if ever, enforced. That's all changed and the ferry ride between Dartmouth and Halifax is still one of the best and least expensive ways to enjoy a harbour cruise. •

• • • The world famous **Cunard Shipping Line** was founded by Halifax native Samuel Cunard. He pioneered the use of steam ships to cross the Atlantic. Critics called his vessels "Iron Steam Kettles" but he proved them wrong by successfully running a service to carry the Royal Mail from England to Halifax in a regular bimonthly run, completing the first of many such voyages in 1840. •

• • • During World War II, Halifax had a military **airport** off Chebucto Road and the naval airport at Shearwater served as the civilian airport until 1960. That year, the Halifax International Airport opened for business. I remember going out to see this new wonder—my first ever visit to an airport. I can't remember what impressed me most—the terminal or taking my first ride on an escalator, which I believe is another first for the province. Not my ride…the escalator! •

Pan American Airways Company field office, Halifax Airport, Chebucto Road, 1931.

A Kill or a Cure

When I was a child in Sherbrooke, I vividly remember a rainy night when my younger cousin was suffering from croup. Relatives drove to Spanish Ship Bay to collect some kind of root. It might have been called flagroot, but no one can recall exactly. It was brought back home, steeped in a tea and given to the baby, who recovered. I've been fascinated with folk medicines ever since.

Clary's great-grandfather, Edward Burns, Sherbrooke, NS, 1964.

• • • **Minards Liniment** was once a staple in almost all Nova Scotian medicine cabinets. It was concocted by Dr. Levi Minard, who practiced medicine in Hants County, Nova Scotia, in the 1860s and prescribed the strong-smelling liniment for his patients. By the 1930s it was known all over the country, and at one time, Minard was the largest seller of any liniment in Canada. Although now produced in Ontario, the main factory used to be in Yarmouth; their ads used to read:

Minards—King of Pain!
Once used—always used!
The old reliable, for man or beast!
A good thing—rub it in!

• • • I remember watching my great-grandfather, Edward Burns, sitting down to a heaping plate of salt cod and pork scraps—liberally sprinkled with more salt— and accompanied by a pasty mixture of dry hot mustard and water with a side of boiled potatoes sprinkled with vinegar. When he finished that meal, he'd go to the medicine cabinet and take a couple of antacids, usually making some remark about their ineffectiveness. Some remedies were expected to work miracles! For years many Nova Scotians have used **mint** to settle an upset tummy and consumed **cod liver oil** as a cure-all for everything from rheumatism to rickets. Today we take our cod liver oil in tablets, but in 1933, the *Halifax Herald* was advertising "Bottled Sunshine" Squibb Cod Liver Oil. It was sold in plain flavour, mint and chocolate coated pills. But that was for wimps. My great-grandfather drank his cod oil straight from the bottle! He died at the age of 91. •

• • • Our early Nova Scotian ancestors had some interesting ideas about curing an **aching tooth**:
Drive a nail in an oak tree or wear the tooth of a corpse around your neck to prevent toothache. Chew on a tea bag to ease a toothache or stop blood after a tooth is pulled.

While the first two suggestions are forms of sympathetic magic and have no physical action on the aching tooth, the belief concerning the use of a tea bag may have some medical credence. It seems the tannic acid in tea leaves acts as a mild coagulant and may help slow the bleeding after an extraction. And here's an interesting sidebar: when John Ritchie of Annapolis Royal died in 1790, he left in his will, among other things, three "teeth brushes." The will didn't stipulate if they were new or used. •

Advertisement for James Lug, Dentist, Sydney, NS, 1866. *Social Reformer*, June 1866.

• • • The November 8, 1791, edition of the *Royal Gazette* carried an advertisement for the services of a man named John Beath, who offered "natural and artificial teeth fixed on gold plates." He also offered "cash for natural teeth," which answers the question of where he got the supplies to make **dentures**. By the Victorian era, things got more scientific—well, sort of. From the *Morning Herald and Commercial Advertiser*, Halifax, March 15, 1841: "Artificial teeth inserted on the principle of atmospheric pressure; warranted for mastication, articulation and beauty. W. Thorn, surgical mechanical dentist, respectfully informs the inhabitants of Halifax and its vicinity, that in addition to his former stock, has just received from England and the United States a supply of incorruptible teeth, which neither corrode nor change colour. Mr. Thorn's method of inserting teeth is not attended with any pain to the patient! And the roots of the decayed teeth are not extracted, and…he dispenses with those wires and ligatures commonly used in his profession, which are injurious to the adjoining teeth …"

A proud boast to say the least, but one not to be outdone by this testimonial from the *Liverpool Transcript*, April 17, 1856: "We have lately seen several specimens of artificial teeth executed by our friend Moore F. Agnew, of this town, who possesses, undoubtedly, the most complete mechanical arrangement of any dentist in this province." •

Simeon Perkins

• • • **Simeon Perkins** was a merchant and politician who lived in Liverpool, Nova Scotia. The diary he kept from 1766 to 1812 provides a fascinating glimpse into early Nova Scotian lifestyles. Records of medical treatment he received are most enlightening: "April 25, 1801: Doctor Webster makes a ointment for my hand of Madeira wine, sweet oil and earthworms…March 16, 1803: My hand is very much swelled, Mr. Kirk advises to wash it with vinegar and wormwood…March 17, 1803: We poultice my hand with flax seed and Indian meal." The treatment didn't seem to do him any harm. Simeon Perkins died on the May 9,1812, apparently of natural causes. •

• • • **Smallpox** killed more young people in the eighteenth century than any other disease, and it took a disastrous toll on the indigenous peoples because they had no resistance to diseases introduced by the newcomers. Back then smallpox was called "yellow fever" or "the pox", and Nova Scotia had several epidemics. A serious one was recorded at Louisbourg in 1755, and it took a heavy toll in Halifax in 1757, 1758 and again in 1799. A somewhat isolated epidemic broke out in Halifax in 1777 among soldiers, who might have contracted it from prisoners of war from the American states. In August and September of 1777, Dr. John Jefferies recorded in his diary that he "…inoculated 127 rebel prisoners of all ages…All of them recovered from the small pox." But inoculation wasn't always accepted by the community. The inoculation procedure, attributed to Dr. Edward Jenner, who first attempted it in 1796, was to introduce a mild form of cowpox or kine pox, which would then give the patient immunity from the more serious smallpox strain. However, some early attempts at inoculation were frequently met with distrust. In fact in 1790, Doctor A. Timothy Miller, who practiced in Liverpool, left because people refused to pay for inoculation—they didn't trust the procedure. •

• • • Have you heard that scientists recently discovered duct tape can help get rid of **warts**? Folk medicine practitioners and scientists alike have been looking for a cure for eons. Sir Kenelm Digby, Gentleman of the Privy Chamber to King Charles the First of England, was a famous scientist and alchemist—some folks say he was a quack. After all, he claimed to have discovered a "powder of sympathy" that could cure a wound from a distance. He also advocated washing hands infected with warts in an empty basin in which the moon shines. So much for science! There is, however, a Nova Scotian belief that advises that washing the wart with water from a stone that holds water. Helen Creighton collected many other folk cures: Rub the wart with a potato or raw meat. Mark a cross on a stove with chalk, one for each wart. The warts will disappear as the chalk burns off. Rub warts with a wedding ring. You can try rubbing the wart with raw meat and throwing it over your shoulder. As the meat rots, the wart goes away. OK, duct tape isn't looking too bad after all! •

• • • When a person was injured and **bleeding** profusely, there were a number of treatments employed by practitioners of folk remedies in Nova Scotia. Cobwebs were often applied to the wound. The sticky spider's web would help stop the blood and hold the cut closed. In Lunenburg County, Helen Creighton was told about a fine dust made from tea and leather that was worked into the cut to stop the bleeding. Others used the yellow blossoms of bloodweed, perhaps a member of the milkweed family. Some people were said to be blood charmers—they could stop blood by using incantations or charms. My own great-aunt, Hannah Burns, was known as a blood charmer in the communities of Sonora and Sherbrooke. Family tradition says she would recite an incantation and hold her hands above the injured area. Several men injured in lumbering accidents were healed in this manner. She intended to pass the secret to my grandmother, but sadly, took it to her grave. •

• • • If cleanliness is truly next to godliness, then **Surprise Soap** must have been thought divine. Many senior Nova Scotians fondly remember this brand of soap, sometimes known as "Shake-Hand Soap" for the picture on the packaging. And it was not just used for cleansing. To cure boils, one could make a paste of this soap mixed with brown sugar and apply it to the affected area. It was a lubricant for hinges, would kill bugs, and often saw service in washing out the mouth of a child who swore. The latter, sadly, I can verify personally. •

• • • Although it can be dangerous if not treated properly, **measles** is no longer the life-threatening disease our Nova Scotian ancestors feared. An ancient Elizabethan remedy for measles was to drink "horse dung water," which is exactly that except the dung was steeped in ale with ginger, treacle and aniseed. Anyway you look at it, it was still horse dung water. Closer to home, Nova Scotians made "nannie tea." Sounds not too bad until you realize it's the same as horse dung water, except the horse dung has been substituted with sheep or "nannie" manure. There was no glossing over the facts at Sherbrooke, where I come from. We called it simply "sheep-shit tea." •

• • • **Baby teeth**—they make children richer and the tooth fairy poorer. The folklore behind the tooth fairy is that by paying for the tooth, it can never be used as a talisman against you. Other tooth lore found in Nova Scotia: a child born with two back teeth is supposed to be a poet. If your teeth grow far apart, you will travel far from home. And cures for a toothache? You might want to try one of these folk remedies collected by Helen Creighton: an Acadian belief advised putting a mustard plaster on your thumb to cure a toothache. A Scottish folk cure from Cape Breton suggested scratching the bad tooth with a splinter from a tree that had been struck by lightning. •

• • • **Molasses** is a delicious sweetener. It also served our ancestors as medicine. We know that sulphur and molasses were used as a spring tonic, but molasses had many other uses. To cure a cold, one could eat a mixture of boiled molasses and onions, or molasses, vinegar, and butter. A common garden shrub, Balm of Gilead, and molasses were boiled together to make a cough syrup. A mixture of teaberries (wintergreen) and molasses made a soothing throat balm. And if you injured yourself and had severe swelling, you could mix yarrow and molasses and apply that to the wound to bring down the inflammation. •

• • • Perhaps the earliest **hospital** in Nova Scotia, the *St. Jean de Dieu*, was operated at Port-Royal in 1629. And in the eighteenth century there was *l' Hôpital du Roy* at Louisbourg. It was a two-storey masonry building with room for one hundred beds and private wards, and was administered by the Brothers of Charity. Early health facilities in Halifax were probably as good as those offered in Europe. Edward Cornwallis brought modern eighteenth-century travelling hospital facilities with him when he founded the city in 1749. The first building was possibly erected just outside the stockade for protection against transmission of diseases. Until the mid-nineteenth century, hospitals were mainly private institutions run for profit. In the 1814 Halifax *Acadian Recorder*, Samuel Head advertised a private hospital for merchant seamen. By 1834, he had three buildings in use and boasted of offering sea baths in the harbour waters with "every attention paid to ventilation and cleanliness." In 1868, the provincial government was petitioned for a hospital to house inebriates. At that time the term didn't necessarily mean drunks; it frequently referred to people suffering from delirium tremors. Many of these poor souls received treatments that must have been horrific. In the old Halifax Hospital, as late as 1927, a coffin-like box that was used to hold one of these unfortunates was found. They would be fed through a hole in the lid and kept immobile, supposedly for their own good. •

Ward 42, Victoria General Hospital, Halifax, NS, c.1910

• • • **Asthma** has become one of modern society's most prevalent diseases. It seems just about every second child carries a puffer or inhaler. Years ago, our Nova Scotian ancestors had folk remedies for this respiratory illness: Stand a child against a door, wall, or even a tree, and bore a hole at his height. Then take a lock of his hair and stop up the hole. As he grows taller than the hole, his asthma will disappear. If that doesn't work try this one: pass the child through a tree that is split and as the split halves grow together, the asthma will fade away. •

• • • Each year thousands of Nova Scotians line up for their annual flu shot. **Influenza** can still take its toll, but we have yet to see a repeat of the disastrous effects of the great Spanish Influenza Epidemic of 1918. It took millions of lives worldwide and hit hard in this province. By early October of 1918, it was in Sydney and Halifax. In Halifax and Dartmouth, public gatherings were banned and by December all schools, churches, and movie houses in Mahone Bay were closed. People looked to some interesting folk beliefs to cure or abate the epidemic. Some wore camphor balls (moth balls), applied a rub of goose grease, inhaled sulphur incense, rubbed on skunk oil, and in extreme cases, had all their teeth extracted. And you worry about a little needle! •

• • • When the cooler weather arrives, many of us suffer from **chapped hands**. There are dozens of creams and lotions on the market today, but our Nova Scotian ancestors had to rely on homemade solutions. A Mi'kmaw remedy uses a liberal coating of bear grease. And according to lore collected by Marion Robertson in Shelburne County, people rubbed their hands with beef tallow or mutton fat. Others made a mild form of lye soap, and after washing their hands with this, rubbed them with white sugar. •

• • • Here's an interesting bit of Shelburne County folklore about **amputation**. An amputated arm must be buried with the fingers straight; if not, the person with the missing arm will suffer pain in the phantom fingers. And here's a tale that is less folk admonishment than bravado. Years ago, I met a man who had a wooden leg. He told me an interesting story, but you be the judge of its validity. He explained that his amputated leg was buried in Dartmouth and he had a burial plot waiting for the rest of him in Halifax; that way when he died, he would be able to straddle the harbour. •

• • • When someone **sneezes**, we often say "God bless you." This comes from the ancient belief that a sneeze opens your soul for a brief moment and evil might enter. A folk rhyme collected by Helen Creighton in Dartmouth gives more detail:
Sneeze on Monday, sneeze for danger
Sneeze on Tuesday, meet a stranger
Sneeze on Wednesday, sneeze for a letter
Sneeze on Thursday, something better
Sneeze on Friday, sneeze for sorrow
Sneeze on Saturday, see your sweetheart tomorrow
It didn't say what happened if you sneezed on Sunday. •

• • • In 1847, surgeons in Edinburgh, Scotland, first used chloroform as an **anesthetic**. Three months later, Halifax doctor William Johnson Almon was the first physician in British North America to use chloroform when he administered it to a female patient before amputating her thumb. One month later, Pictou chemist J.D.B. Fraser administered some homemade chloroform to his wife to ease her pain during childbirth. •

Love, Life and Death

How can you explain love? Who knows the mysteries of death? If I had the answers I'd be a rich man. What am I saying? I adore my wife. I have a wonderful, loving family and dear friends, and when I die my ashes will be scattered on the sea surrounding my beloved Nova Scotia. I am a rich man!

Gravestone iconography, Old Burying Ground, Halifax

Here lies Interr'd the Bodies of the Children

• • • In years gone by, Nova Scotians of Celtic ancestry marked the occasion of a **funeral** with customs we seldom see today. The body was "waked" in the house, and it was common for a group of men to stay awake all night in a death vigil that was almost always accompanied by strong drink. Custom maintained that the corpse had to be carried to its grave; it was considered an act of disrespect to have a horse or hearse carry it to its final resting place. A piper led the procession, followed by the mourners and behind them, a man appointed to carry the jug to fortify the assembly along the route. •

• • • Halifax, 1750—one year after the city was founded, a civil suit was brought to court. It was the case of Lieutenant William Williams and Amy Williams, the later as respondent. Williams brought several witnesses to prove his wife's adultery with Thomas Thomas, who had no charges brought against him. The husband was granted divorce with permission to marry again. The former Mrs. William Williams was forbidden to marry as long as her ex-husband lived, and she was to leave the province within ten days. This was the first recorded **divorce** in Canada. •

Clary and Sharon Croft on their wedding day, March 3, 1972.

• • • Getting **married** is sometimes called "tying the knot." Women in ancient Rome wore love knots tied around their waist which their new husbands would symbolically untie—untying the garter is a holdover from this custom. At Clark's Harbour on Nova Scotia's western shore, a man would send love knots to his intended, and she would untie the knot or move it on the string if she wanted him. I guess there really is nothing new under the sun! •

• • • As early as 1849, lobsters were being canned in small factories throughout Nova Scotia. Many of the early lobster factories were really just sheds used to cook and can the shelled meat. Since there was no refrigeration, workers had to finish the day's catch before their shift ended. For women, working in a lobster factory was one of the first forms of employment outside the home, and many a love match was made by swains and maids at the factory. In fact, my wife's grandparents Christina May Richard and Seymour Brown met and **fell in love** while working in a lobster factory on Pictou Island. •

• • • In the Nova Scotia of 1857, a husband could be granted a divorce on grounds of adultery, while his wife needed a second reason in addition to adultery. The reason given for the discrepancy was that husbands were just being men. "An adulterous husband…was simply following his 'natural' desires." Think that seems odd? Read on. In the nineteenth century, a bizarre form of divorce was practised in Great Britain and also in Nova Scotia. It was known as **wife sale** and was apparently a recognized option until 1899. It worked this way: a man could "sell" or transfer the rights of marriage between himself and his wife to another man. According to the Halifax *Daily Echo* of November 2, 1889, a sailor "agreed to formalize the transfer of his wife and children for forty dollars." There was no comment on what the wife thought of the deal. •

Admiral Digby's Well, First well in Digby, Nova Scotia.

• • • Ever drop a coin into a **wishing well**? Did your wish come true? In ancient times it was common to drop a stone into a well to forecast the future. If the water bubbled, the outcome would look good; if it clouded, it looked bad. When coins became common, rocks were gradually replaced with money. Here in Nova Scotia, Helen Creighton collected this belief in Clark's Harbour: drop a ball of yarn down a well, holding one end and say:

> **We'll wind and we'll bind,**
> **Our true love to find,**
> **The colour of his hair and**
> **the clothes he'll wear,**
> **The day that he weds to me.**

Try that at your local shopping mall fountain and see how far you get! •

• • • **Funeral customs** are, well, a part of life. The early European settlers to Nova Scotia brought their own rituals to the funeral service and style of mourning. In Lunenburg County some funerals were conducted according to the customs prevailing in Germany; especially at a child's funeral, artificial flowers made by girls and fashioned into wreaths were carried in the procession. The funerals of some prominent people were held at St. Paul's Anglican Church in Halifax. On November 11, 1782, Michael Franklin, the former lieutenant-governor, was given a magnificent public funeral and interred in the vault at the left of the altar. Accounts tell of more than two hundred Mi'kmaw participants chanting the death song as they followed the coffin to its final resting place. When Baron de Sietz, colonel and chief of a regiment of Hessian foot soldiers, died in Halifax on December 19, 1782, he was buried under St. Paul's. The late baron was clothed in full military dress, sword by his side, spurs upon his feet, and an orange in his hand, following the ancient German feudal tradition when the last baron of a noble house dies. •

• • • Funeral customs in Nova Scotia continue to change as each century unfolds. Most people today work with a **funeral home** for the final arrangements of a departed loved one. It wasn't that way in eighteenth-century Louisbourg. Records from the period 1713 to 1758 show that there were no funeral parlors at the fortress or town. The corpse was waked in the home and then carried to the chapel for a service, followed by a procession to the town graveyard. And if custom at Louisbourg followed that of France, women didn't join the funeral procession—it was a male-only ritual. •

• • • During the nineteenth- and early twentieth-centuries, **autograph books** were extremely popular, especially with young women. These books frequently included flowery or humorous verses swearing everlasting love—platonic friendship or sometimes even more. A delightful autograph book owned by Mary Chisholm and housed at the Nova Scotia Archives and Record Management contains several verses extolling various forms of love. Mary collected the entries from friends around the province and at her school, the Convent of the Sacred Heart, in Halifax. Here are a few of them:

Do not forget my seventeenth birthday, how I carried a cloud in the morning, and in the afternoon a ray of sunshine, of course you know why?
October 20, 1879. C.E.J.O.C.

The rose is red, the violet blue, The pink is pretty, and so are you.
Your sincere friend,
Bessie Fuller

Love is like Scotch snuff One pinch and that's enough.
Mary J., 1881

The humble lines which here I trace Years may not change nor age efface They may be read though valued not When the one who penned [them] is forgot.
James K. Kelleher, 1878 •

• • • Anyone who has ever been through it will tell you that planning a **wedding** is far more difficult than it first appears. Deciding to get married is easy; planning the wedding ceremony is a true test of any relationship. But if you think modern weddings are hard to plan, think what some our Nova Scotian ancestors had to contend with. Couples living in remote areas of the province had to wait for a visiting clergyman. In the eighteenth century the provincial secretary Richard Bulkeley wrote to Isaac deChamp, a justice of the peace in Kings County, and warned him that he didn't have the right to perform marriages, and if he persisted he would risk prosecution. Enoch Towner was a churchwarden in the episcopal church in Digby during the latter part of the eighteenth century. He changed to the "New Light" religion espoused by Henry Alline and began pastoral duties. By law all marriages in Nova Scotia had to be performed by a clergyman of the Church of England; contrary to that law, Towner married Jacob Cornwall to Sarah Titus in Digby in 1800. The townsfolk were irate. The miscreant reverend was thrown out of town and had fish guts, eggs and mud thrown after him. He was brought to trial in Halifax but was vindicated when it was decreed ministers of any Christian faith could perform wedding ceremonies. •

• • • In love, where there's a will there's a way. Take as an example couples who want to get **married** against the wishes of their parents. Had they lived in eighteenth-century Louisbourg, they could have been joined together "à la gaumine," whereby a couple went together to mass and waited until the moment just before the priest gave the general benediction, at which time they pronounced themselves aloud to be husband and wife. In other parts of the province an English ceremony allowed couples to enjoy the privileges of a married couple while waiting for the visit of traveling clergy. Known as a "holdfast ceremony," it took place when a couple stood in the presence of their community and proclaimed themselves married. They would be joined formally when the next visiting clergyman came by. •

• • • **Television reality shows** featuring odd or unusual weddings seem to have fairly wide popularity these days. I wonder how they'd deal with some of the weddings from past years in Nova Scotia? Years ago, when couples often had to wait until a minister visited their area, it wasn't uncommon for the opportunist clergyman to go into high gear with a fire and brimstone sermon as part of the marriage ceremony. After all, he had a full house and a captive crowd! A quaint kind of equine-inspired wedding ceremony took place at Truro late in the eighteenth century. The bride's party and the groom's party would meet on horseback, circle each other and pass a bottle of grog. Then they would ride back together to the wedding ceremony. In the early nineteenth century, the Reverend Doctor MacGregor ministered to folks living in Pictou County. He was once obliged to perform a ceremony in two languages; the groom spoke only English and the bride spoke what some in Pictou County called the original language of the Garden of Eden—Gaelic. MacGregor later said, "I had to tell the man his duties in English and the woman hers in Gaelic. How they managed to court or converse afterwards I know not." When United Empire Loyalist widower the Reverend John Wiswall moved to Wilmot, Nova Scotia, he decided to take a new wife. The bride, herself a widowed Loyalist, was a Mrs. Hutchinson. The ceremony was performed by a Mr. Baley, who spoke of his colleague being "united in the holy bonds of matrimony to the rib of his choice." •

Occupations and Crafts

I am so fortunate to do work I love. I always tell young people to find something they will do for free and then find a way to get paid doing it. But I realize not everyone can be that lucky!

• • • The **hospitality industry** is one of Nova Scotia's most important businesses. We boast some world-class lodgings and are known for our genuine hospitality. And that's nothing new.

Beginning in the 1840s, the Stag Inn at Preston was operated by George Dear, then by William Dear and his wife. A sign over the door, inscribed with a verse written by a patron, Captain (later Colonel) William Chearnley read:

The "Stag Hotel" is kept by William Dear,
Outside, the House looks somewhat queer,
Only Look-in, and there's no fear,
But you'll find Inside, the best of Cheer,
Brandy, Whiskey, Hop, Spruce, Ginger Beer,
Clean Beds, and food for Horses here:
Round about, both far and near,—
Are Streams for Trout, and Woods for Deer,
To suit the Public taste,—'tis clear,—
Bill Dear will Labour,
so will his dearest dear. •

Sign, Stag Hotel

• • • If all the tales of buried treasure can be believed, **pirates** were once as plentiful as flies along Nova Scotia's coast. But theirs' was a risky occupation. If caught, they could be hanged, covered in tar, and hung in a metal cage as a warning to others. Halifax's famed Hangman's Beach on McNab's Island at the mouth of the harbour is named after such practices. Another hanging place was at Point Pleasant Park, also at the harbour's entrance. Some time during the eighteenth century, a pirate by the name of Jordan was hanged in Halifax. His body was covered in tar so it wouldn't be picked at by the birds—not out of respect for the corpse, but to keep it around longer. Then it was placed in an iron cage and suspended near a spot now called Black Rock. The grisly corpse remained there as a warning until it frightened the lieutenant-governor's lady, who was out riding. •

Studio pirate drama in costume for skating carnival, Exhibition Building, Halifax, NS, c.1885.

• • • 78—ring—4. That was our telephone number in Sherbrooke when I was a kid in the early 1950s. Back then the **telephone** was a large wooden box suspended on the wall, featuring a mouthpiece for speaking and a receiver for listening—the latter the most interesting on a party line. We'd think it odd if the phone company (or communications provider, as we say these days) were to tell us when we could make a call, but back in 1909 when the Antigonish and Sherbrooke Telephone Company had its head offices in Sherbrooke, their directory not only warned patrons not to use the telephone during thunder storms, but reminded them, "It is expected that Sunday calls…will be necessary ones only." And remember when your elders used to say the snowfall was so heavy it reached the tops of the power poles? They were probably right. The Abercrombie Rural Mutual Telephone Company was formed in 1914. Local men were paid fifty cents for each pole hole dug. The poles were only fourteen feet high—the same height as telegraph poles. •

• • • With the proliferation of cell phones, it's hard to imagine a time without telephone communication. Nova Scotians were on the leading edge of phone service, perhaps because Alexander Graham Bell made his summer home in Cape Breton. In 1888 there were seven hundred phones in Nova Scotia and by 1905, there were thirty **phone companies** in the province. In 1904, the telephone company in Dartmouth was housed in a residence on Edward Street. Two rooms were used for the switchboard, and the switchboard operator was then known as the "Hello Girl." •

• • • At one time there were many **peddlers** traveling the roads and seacoasts of Nova Scotia. One of the most famous was a man named Peter Smith. Born in Dublin in 1800, he left Ireland for Nova Scotia at the age of seventeen. He spent his early years in Guysborough County as a peddler, selling needles, pins, and ribbon, and carrying his wares on his back. Later he operated stores in Cape Breton. He had a reputation for not giving away too many bargains. In fact, he's remembered in folklore for a famous Gaelic curse put upon him, which in English translates as follows: "May he fall off the bridge, and may the lobsters devour his tender parts." •

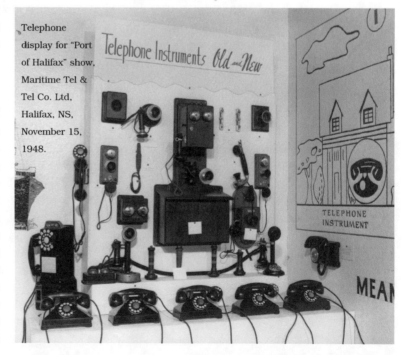

Telephone display for "Port of Halifax" show, Maritime Tel & Tel Co. Ltd, Halifax, NS, November 15, 1948.

• • • In these days of huge container ships, it's hard to realize the importance **barrels** once played in shipping Nova Scotia's resources around the world. Barrels were used to ship flour, fish, molasses, rum, and fruit. Produce barrels were called "dry" barrels; fish and rain barrels were "wet." Until 1863, it was primarily fish barrels that were made in Nova Scotia. Then a man from the Annapolis Valley came down to Lunenburg County and ordered a number of barrels for the apple industry. He sold them for fifty cents apiece—and a good crop of apples in the valley could use two million barrels. Over the years, millions of barrels filled with apples were shipped to England, until the shippers requested square boxes to fit better in the ships' holds. •

Minature market basket made by Edith Clayton.

• • • Nova Scotian crafts have been recognized around the world as some of the finest of their kind. In the African Nova Scotian community, the tradition of **basket-making** has been passed on from generation to generation. Its most respected and famous craftswoman was Edith Clayton. She carried on a tradition brought from the United States during the War of 1812 from black slaves and immigrants who left the area around Chesapeake Bay. In Nova Scotia, this style of basket has been sold at the Halifax City Market since the mid 1800s, when the market was at Cheapside and Bedford Row. Descendants and relatives of Mrs. Clayton, including her sister Nancy Lucas and her daughter Clara Gough, still proudly carry on the craft of making beautiful baskets and other containers. These products can still be found at markets in Halifax and Dartmouth. •

• • • Rug or **mat-hooking** is an old craft in Nova Scotia. From 1892 until recently, *Bluenose* patterns from John E. Garrett, Ltd. in New Glasgow were available for folks who didn't produce their own designs. Many of these mats still grace the floors and walls of Maritime homes. For a number of years these rugs were bought at markets or directly off the floors of the homes of the makers by the famous (or infamous) "Yankee Peddlers," who exchanged the beautiful hand-hooked mats for shiny new linoleum. While some decried the exploitation of the craftspeople, who received only a fraction of the value realized when the mat was sold to a collector or buyer in the "Boston States," many of the rug-makers considered it a good deal. My grandmother Maxine MacKay sold many rugs to the peddlers. She said folks could always make a rug, but they couldn't manufacture the store-bought floor coverings. She knew the mats were being sold for a hefty profit, but told me she believed she got value for her time and effort. •

Rug hooked in 2003 by my mother, Olive Croft.

• • • In eighteenth- and nineteenth-century Nova Scotia, most rural households could claim the owner- ship of at least one **spinning wheel**. Used to spin linen or wool into thread, the large wheels were known as walking wheels while the smaller sit-down spinners were known as flax wheels. Nova Scotia had several well-known spinning-wheel manufacturers; many were small cottage industries. They were run by people like Alexander Macintosh at Pictou, Hector Fraser at Baddeck, and the Young (Yung) family in Lunenburg County, whose wheels were known for their distinctive red and black wood bands. •

• • • **Weaving cloth** was once a common household chore for both men and women in Nova Scotia. The basic Acadian loom had two shafts for sim- ple weaving, four shafts being introduced in the nine- teenth century. The shaft is the part that holds the threads and separates them to allow the shuttle to pass through. Many people bought the warp (the length) of cotton at the store and wove the weft (the width) from linen or wool that they manufactured on their own farms. If they had extra, they would weave material to sell. In the 1930s, weavers in Cape Breton would make thirty yards of blanket material at a time and sell it for ten cents per yard. •

Traditional overshot pattern "Sun, Moon and Stars" coverlet woven by Clary Croft.

• • • Most early **Victorian women** did not work outside the home, but the advance of the Industrial Revolution expanded opportunities and changed the way business was carried out. Still, the *Ladies Home Journal* of 1900 wrote: "It is a plain, simple fact that women have shown themselves naturally incompetent to fill a great many of the business positions which they have sought to occupy…" This was obviously the feeling in many Nova Scotian businesses as well. A male clerk at the office of the General Mining Association in Sydney earned $600 per year in 1901—that was $165 a year above the average miner's wage. A woman doing a similar clerking job would make less than the male miner. •

• • • There's a lot of talk of **brain drain** these days, but it's nothing new. Between 1870 and 1900, 250,000 Maritimers—forty percent of the population—moved away, mostly to the United States. By 1870 more than six thousand Nova Scotians had settled in Boston and by 1880, there were more Nova Scotians in Boston than in Yarmouth, Sydney and Pictou combined. In the 1890s, 93,000 people left the Maritimes. The *Shelburne Budget* of 1899 wrote: "Let the traveller go into the homes of people in towns and country, and he will see in nine homes out of ten the photograph of some absent boy, who is prospering under the Stars and Stripes." •

• • • Halifax was home to the first **newspaper** in Canada: the *Halifax Gazette*. The first printing office was set up in a shop on Grafton Street in 1751 by Bartholomew Green, Jr., whose father had earlier established Boston's first paper. Young Green came to Halifax to found the paper but died soon after his arrival. His venture fell to his friend John Bushell. On March 23, 1752, Bushell issued the first edition, which consisted of four small pages the size of a sheet of foolscap folded. The masthead carried a woodcut of a man hunting fowl and another of a ship in full sail. It carried only two advertisements: one for a man offering his legal services, and another rather long entry from Proctor and Scutt near the North Gate. They sold butter and also offered lessons in "spelling, reading, writing in all its different hands, arithmetic, the true Italian method of bookkeeping" and "any of the arts and sciences." Appropriately enough, you could find them at the sign of the Hand and Pen. •

Halifax Gazette April 6, 1752.

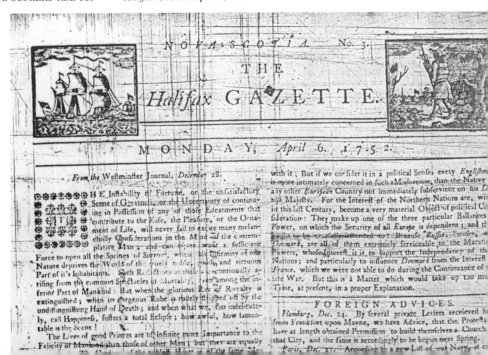

• • • **As times change**, so do the types of businesses once found in a major seaport town such as Halifax. For example, by 1950, the Halifax firm of Bentley & Fleming was up for sale after 189 years in business. They were major manufacturers of spars for sailing vessels, a commodity not often used by modern vessels. Halifax also had its share of blacksmiths.

In 1909, Robinson's Livery Stables on Doyle Street advertised that they catered to city visitors. But livery stables and blacksmiths catering to livestock lost considerable business when automobiles became popular. As in all businesses, it was adapt or perish. After all, you don't see too many stores selling eight-track tapes, do you? •

• • • In earlier times, many **post offices** in rural Nova Scotia were operated from private homes. A fascinating account of the rural post office in the home of Miss Nellie Mahar and her brother Charlie in Glen Margaret in the 1920s is written in an unpublished remembrance by Rowena Neil Watson, who summered at Glen Margaret with her family. She remembered how Charlie would bring the mail from the train at the French Village station, and every day, people would line up at the door while Nellie sorted the mail in her kitchen. The opened door was the signal to go in and collect the mail, which was arranged on the kitchen table. And sitting erect at that table in

George MacQueen, Blacksmith in Shubenacadie, 1907.

a white, starched blouse and apron was Nellie, staring over her spectacles. The letters for residents of the area were arranged in alphabetical order; the Halifax newspapers wrapped in brown paper. Stamps were kept in an old wooden cigar box, and the post mistress kept a tiny pot of water and a sponge for wetting the required postage. She ran her business with efficiency and no frills. As Rowena wrote, "There was absolutely no joviality in that kitchen. Miss Mahar was a government employee, an official on duty. Her account books were almost like works of art, each numeral and letter perfectly formed." And if the post office was closed? No problem. One of the small panes in her kitchen window had been removed and replaced by a tin box with a slot in it. Patrons could drop their letters through this slot. If they didn't have a stamp, they could leave the correct change, and Nellie would make sure the mail had the proper postage attached. •

Post Office, Sherbrooke Village Restoration, 1974. Once a private home that also housed the post office. My Aunt Estella Gillen ran a tea room out of this building.

French Village Station. Charlie Mahar in double-seater waiting for the mail and passengers, Tantallon, Nova Scotia, c.1915.

• • • **Windmills** were once common on the Nova Scotia landscape. An 1817 drawing of a windmill at Pictou shows a structure very similar to those seen in the Netherlands today. However, governments had restrictions placed on their construction and repair, as is evidenced in a December 30, 1820, petition put before the provincial government. In a sworn statement, John Albro of Dartmouth stated that he was the owner of a windmill damaged by wind and requested permission to import parts from the United States to make the repairs. The mill has long since gone, but the name of Dartmouth's Windmill Road recognizes the legacy. •

"View of Halifax, Nova Scotia from the Red Mill, Dartmouth, c.1853."Artist: Robert D. Wilkie; Engraver: P. Mayor. From *Gleason's Illustrated Magazine*, September 10, 1853.

• • • The word **midwife** comes from Old English—"with woman." The first European midwife in Halifax was Ann Medlicot, who arrived with Edward Cornwallis in 1749. Ten years later, Mrs. Ann Catherwood, who was appointed as a midwife by the board of trade in the early days of Halifax, retired because of ailing health. However, the government recommended that she receive a pension for her years of midwifery service. For years, skilled midwives were respected members of the community; however, by the latter part of the nineteenth century, the medical profession was beginning to lobby against midwifery. By 1872, women practising in Halifax had to have a certificate from the provincial medical board. This didn't seem to have been necessary in rural areas, perhaps because less attention was given to births by the authorities. My mother was brought into the world with the assistance of a midwife and my great-grandmother, Cora Burns, acted as midwife for numerous families. These women obviously took little heed of the opinions found in a 1910 report published in the *Halifax Herald* that stated, "[Midwives]…ignorant, coarse, irresponsible, go to the homes of the poorer class, and there is not the slightest doubt that their administrations are due in large measure [to] the class of evils which have engaged the enlightenment of men of medical profession and trained nurses everywhere." •

Midwife Cora (McDiarmid) Burns, Sherbrooke, 1964.

• • • Someone looking for a high-profile career in eighteenth-century Nova Scotia might take on the job of **drummer**. Drummers at Fortress Louisbourg in Cape Breton were considered among the elite of the military. They were given better food and lodging than the average soldier, and, aside from their pay, they were kept in linen and shoes, as long as they maintained their drum skins taut and their drumsticks in excellent condition. (Not always an easy feat in the constant fog of Louisbourg.) We know of one Louisbourg drummer named Pierre Boziac who also earned extra money as a dancing instructor. •

• • • In Victorian Halifax, the Halifax **Boot and Shoe Factory**, owned and operated by George Yates, operated out of premises on George Street. They advertised "Boots and shoes…from the kind destined to skim along the drawing room, to the sort fitted to tread the greasy slippery decks of a fishing vessel…" They also boasted that their business "gives employment to a considerable number of workers, both male and female, most of whom make reasonable remunerative wages, while the more skilled realize very handsome pay." •

• • • **Taverns** abounded in the eighteenth- and nineteenth- centuries and were often operated by widows as one of the few legal enterprises open to them. Some early Nova Scotian settlers received land grants on the condition that they open and operate taverns for travellers—long before ready accommodations were available. In 1749, the year Halifax was founded, twenty tavern licenses were issued for the new settlement. Most served meals. John O'Brien's British Coffee House offered "beef soup or mutton broth everyday at 12 o'clock until the weather grows warm." But levels of service and cleanliness were variable. By 1783, taverns were governed by a standards law, but the standards were not always acceptable. The bishop of Nova Scotia once described how he was forced to sleep on the tavern floor to avoid bed bugs. •

• • • The production of **salt cod** once employed many Nova Scotians. During the peak years of production, from the turn of the nineteenth century until the 1930s, Newfoundland was the leader in salt cod manufacturing, followed by Lunenburg County in Nova Scotia. The cod was split and salted, then placed on huge racks called flakes to dry in the sun. There were flakes all over the countryside up until the 1920s, when most of the commercial drying began to be done with mechanical dryers indoors. But it must have been wonderful to see flakes covering the waterfronts, including Halifax and what is now the site of the Bluenose Golf Club at Lunenburg. •

Fish flakes, Lunenburg County.

• • • Nova Scotia was once home to hundreds of small **tanning** businesses. In the nineteenth century, there were three tanneries in Bayfield that supplied finished leather for shoemakers, harness-makers, and anyone else who required it. Farmers and trappers would bring their animal hides to the tanner; the hides were put into lime pits, then into a salt solution. Both of these processes were done mainly to remove the hair. Last, the hides were placed in a vat containing a hemlock-based solution to soften, cure, and colour the skins. But while they supplied a necessary commodity and a large number of jobs, tanneries weren't popular in urban areas, primarily because of the smell and pollution to the waterways. Barnstead's Tannery on Spring Garden Road in Halifax in the 1870s was removed once residents began complaining about the smell. •

• • • From colonial times, **milk** was delivered to individual homes, but for a number of those early years people had to provide their own containers. Milk vendors carried pint and quart measures and filled the receptacle. In turn-of-the-century Halifax, milk was delivered to certain homes by two elderly women who made their deliveries from pails yoked over their shoulders. Many times children were employed in home delivery. At Halifax in the 1880s, Alex Bond sold his milk from steel oblong boxes fitted with padlocks. But times were changing and people wanted a more sanitary method of milk delivery. An announcement in the *Halifax Morning Chronicle* on May 18, 1885, stated that Alex Bond, well-known dairyman on Kaye Street in Halifax, had begun the first deliveries of bottled milk from his dairy at Shubenacadie. The paper wrote, "This system has given universal satisfaction in London, [England], New York and Montreal, Canada..." •

BOTTLED MILK.—Mr. Alex. Bond, the well-known dairyman, of 44 Kaye street, this city, has launched his enterprise of serving his customers with bottled milk, put up at his dairy at Shubenacadie, and has won praise for the start he has made and the quality of the article. He says the cost of starting is great, and such as will make a complete failure, if not a complete success. The following from his circular explains the idea: He intends delivering pure, fresh, country milk to retail customers in glass jars (or bottles) of two sizes, viz., pints and quarts (under regulations as per accompanying card). This system has given universal satisfaction in London, E., New York, and Montreal, Canada, and we firmly believe has only to receive a fair trial to commend itself to consumers generally. The advantages are many, among which may be mentioned these, viz.: All dust, &c., is excluded, the bottles are perfectly airtight, and hence it is claimed that the milk will retain its sweetness and delicious flavor much longer than under the old system.

Notice of bottled milk production by Alex Bond. *Morning Chronicle*, May 18, 1885.

• • • We tend to think of the **captains** of tall ships as men, but now and then, women did take the helm. Here's one tale with a local connection to prove the point: After smallpox left the crew and the captain of the *Rothesay* unable to handle the ship, the captain's daughter, Bessie Hall, navigated the vessel from Florida to Liverpool, England, in 1870. She made one more voyage in 1871, then retired from the sea to marry and raise a family in Annapolis County, Nova Scotia. •

Bessie Hall with her father, Captain Joseph Hall.

• • • Halifax was once home to a large **cotton factory**. Opened in 1883, the Nova Scotia Cotton Manufacturing Company was housed in a three-storey building located in the city's north end on Robie Street (today, the Piercy's Building Supplies lot). The business and factory were acquired by Dominion Cotton Mills (later Dominion Textiles) of Montreal in 1891 and at the time of its takeover, the company was the second largest in Halifax with 317 employees. In that year men earned $7.50 a week, women $3.90, and children $1.25. The factory was destroyed by fire in the aftermath of the Halifax Explosion in 1917. •

• • • When you buy live **lobsters** at the store today, they come with their claws bound with elastic. This is to protect you from getting pinched but also to prevent the lobsters from hurting each other in the holding tanks. In fact, here's a tip from my father-in-law, who was a lobster fisherman for years: never buy lobsters from a tank if some are missing antennae. It means they have probably been there for a long time and have begun to cannibalize each other. Not too many years ago, lobster fishermen used to stop up the lobsters' claws with tiny wooden pegs called lobster plugs. Made of pine, these plugs had to be fashioned with a slight curve to fit the seam in the lobster's claw. When the weather was bad and the boats couldn't get out to set traps, many fishermen would sit and chat while they whittled thousands of plugs. •

• • • Nova Scotia is still experimenting with **Sunday shopping**. And for the present, we can expect the debate to go on. But this is nothing new. In 1896 an evangelical rally was held in the Dartmouth Rink to stir up support against what the preachers called "unnecessary Sunday labour." One of their targets was barber shops, which used to be open on Sunday mornings to allow barbers to shave their customers before church. •

• • • **Aquaculture** is a multi-million dollar industry in Nova Scotia. Not only do we farm mussels and oysters, we breed and grow salmon, trout, and several species of exotic fish. It's possible we may have had the first example of aqua-farming in North America. In 1604, Samuel de Champlain wrote of planting gardens outside the fort at Port-Royal and surrounding one of those gardens with ditches. The ditches were then filled with water and housed live trout, ready for the settler's dinner table. •

• • • **Educators** are one of our most valuable resources and should be paid accordingly, but it seems we have had a long and undistinguished history of poor recognition of our teachers—especially women teachers. In Dartmouth at the turn of the nineteenth century, the average female school teacher could expect to teach for 212 days and be paid around $275 per year. The principal, invariably a man, received considerably more: $1000 per year. And if teachers wanted a raise they would have to prove that their students' grades reflected the quality of their teaching. •

The Unusual

When people find out I work in the field
of folklore, they often say, "I bet you know
some great ghost stories!" I do.
But it isn't merely tales of ghosts that
I find interesting and unusual.
There are many unexplained things
to discover in Nova Scotia.

• • • Seen anything **odd in the waters** off Nova Scotia lately? We used to! On July 15, 1825, a strange creature was seen in Halifax Harbour by several people. Its "body [was] as big as a tree trunk—the animal had about eight coils or humps to its body and it was about sixty feet long." And on July 7, 1890, the *Halifax Morning Chronicle* wrote about an odd sighting off Lunenburg: "The sea serpent put in his appearance here a few days ago. It was seen by a number of fishermen while employed in overhauling their nets, and we are informed there was a stampede. It was also seen by a gentleman from town, who states that it was upwards of sixty yards long and at the time was leisurely propelling itself along the surface of the harbour." •

• • • One of Halifax's most famous **ghost dwellings** is the house with the mysterious black window. Located on Robie Street and built in the 1840s, the window is on the south side of the house facing Jubilee Road. There are many legends as to why the window is black, but one factor in the tradition remains consistent: It is said that no matter how often the glass in the window is replaced it soon turns black. Some say a man looked out the window and spied witches dancing on the verandah. They stopped when they saw him but bewitched the window black. Another story has a man cleaning his gun when it went off; the bullet flew through the window and shot a boy who was playing in a tree. And the truth? While I was studying folklore at Saint Mary's University in 1976, I was curious about these tales and decided to investigate. I simply knocked on the door and was told by the owner that the window represents nothing more than an attempt at architectural symmetry. The design is classic Greek revival, and to ensure three openings on each side of the building, the designers planned three windows on three sides. (The front has two windows and a door.) However, on the south side they needed an interior wall that would run into the centre of the middle window. The solution? Create a false exterior window and paint it black! •

Black window, 2004.

• • • Halifax's Neptune Theatre has its own resident ghost. The theatre's staff call him **Syd from the Grid**. Some say he is a sailor who fell from the grid or flies. Others say he is an old vaudeville actor who was angry when the theatre was turned into a movie house and has come back to be part of the legitimate theatre world. Whatever the reason, Syd has made his presence known to a few theatre folks over the years. Former house manager Keith MacPhail and the crew chief were closing up the bar one night when they heard the chain around the bar fridge rattle, though no one was near it. Another time, actor and head of Neptune's Theatre School Jennette White and her sister were working late one night when they heard footsteps on the roof. They called the police and a search was conducted. No one was found. Two people from the box office believe they might have seen Syd standing at the centre of the stage. They called the police, and the theatre was searched, but, again, no one was found. Perhaps strangest of all—former head carpenter Jack Blackmore was doing a set-up on stage by himself. He heard footsteps come down the aisle and saw seat A1 drop down then go back up. Then he heard footsteps go back up and leave the house. I may have experienced Syd myself. Once, while performing in *A Midsummer Night's Dream*, I and several other members of the cast heard a strange noise in the flies as if someone was walking about above our heads. The stage manager sent the crew chief up to do a safety inspection, but she found nothing. Perhaps it's more than fitting that one of the classic lines from that play is "Oh what fools these mortals be!" •

• • • St. Paul's Anglican Church on Halifax's Grand Parade is Canada's oldest Protestant church. It's a handsome structure that since 1750 has been a much-loved and admired part of the city. Naturally, its most important role is as an Anglican church, but for many residents and visitors, its most distinguishing feature is the famous window with the **outline of a man's head**. One myth concerning the origin of this profile silhouette is that the blast from the 1917 Halifax Explosion decapitated the rector and his head flew through the window, leaving only the eerie image. But the true tale is less macabre. The image did, apparently, appear as a result of the Halifax Explosion, but the cause was nothing more than the glass being shattered into this unusual shape. In fact, one look at the window would tell you that if the legend of the decapitation were true, the rector would have been a giant, such is the size of the silhouette. •

St Paul's Anglican Church, Halifax. Window with image taken from church interior.

• • • For some unaccountable reason, Nova Scotia has been host to many **UFO sightings**. In the eighteenth century, Simeon Perkins reported seeing unexplained lights in the sky over Liverpool. From the *Journal of Proceedings of the Provincial Establishment on Sable Island* comes this September 22, 1842, diary entry by Joseph Darby: "Two men came up this morning from the south side house where they stayed all night. They saw a strange and unusual light about two miles to the westward of the little house…it used to appear above the land about 6 or 8 feet, in a large bright light about the bulk of a large pot, and incline downward until it touched the land, all the time diminishing in size until it disappeared on the surface of the land. In a few seconds again it would be large and bright above the land, descend slowly, diminishing in size until it was lost…on the surface of the land. This was repeated five or six times in the same spot and within the space of about five minutes. To this James Jackson and Martin Clye [sic] are willing to swear." But perhaps the most famous sighting took place in October 1967 off Shag Harbour, in Shelburne County. According to an article in the March 26, 1975, edition of the *4th Estate*, "Many people saw a lighted object, 60 feet in diameter, descend toward the ocean. Moments later several local RCMP constables confirmed the presence of the object resting on the water 2-3 hundred yards offshore." Several fishing vessels and a coast guard cutter were dispatched to the scene, but the object was gone by the time of their arrival. All that was left was a forty yard wide patch of yellow foam. The sighting remains a mystery to this day and has attracted international attention. •

• • • Ghosts and theatres make good companions. At the Bauer Theatre in Antigonish, there is a **ghost named "Harold"** or "Hector." The folk tale surrounding his hauntings is that years ago a St. Francis Xavier University student boxer named Hector was knocked unconscious and died; other versions say he was running track and dropped dead from a heart attack. (This was the alleged reason for boxing being banned as a sport at that university.) I spoke to some folks at the university who told me the ghost has been experienced in the theatre, and an actor friend Cliff LeJeune told me that in 1977, during a production of *Jesus Christ Superstar*, he believes he heard "Hector" running on the track beside the theatre. •

• • • When Helen Creighton began collecting folk songs and tales of the supernatural in 1928, her initial contacts were made at Eastern Passage, at the mouth of Halifax Harbour. One of the first families to share their lore was the Hartlans. Enos Hartlan and his wife made Helen feel comfortable and welcome, and soon invited her to use their home as a temporary office, and set up her notebooks on their kitchen table. But during her first visit Dr. Creighton noticed something peculiar. Written on a board attached above the main entrance door were nine letters—**UDWWFUWUU**. These nine letters represented the first letters of each word of the German phrase *Und das Wort ward fleisch und wohnte unter uns*. The English translation of this Bible verse from John 4:14 is *And the Word was made flesh and dwelt among us*. Enos Hartlan later explained to Dr. Creighton that with these holy letters above the door, a witch could not enter their house. •

• • • Along Halifax's Bedford Highway, the music rotunda from Prince's Lodge is still visible. The only remaining structure of the former estate of Edward, Duke of Kent, the lodge is situated near the site of a very strange occurrence that began with a duel in July 1796. The Duke of Kent and his companion, Julie St. Laurent, were entertaining a visiting baron and holding a large card party on the lawns. An argument arose between two of the duke's officers, Colonel Ogilvie and Captain Howard, and they fought a **duel** with sabers. Howard killed Ogilvie, but died soon after from wounds. The duke was outraged and refused the men a military funeral. He ordered them buried nearby in unmarked graves. Years later when the railroad was being cut through the old property at the Prince's Lodge, two skeletons were discovered. The excavations disturbed the hidden graves and now, on certain nights, some people claim see the men, once again, dueling with swords. •

Prince's Lodge, music room

• • • Sometimes tales of the supernatural prove to have ordinary explanations. Such is the case in a story told in 1925 to folklore collector Arthur Fauset by Clarence Marie, a longshoreman living in Yarmouth. Clarence's family moved to a house that had a reputation for being **haunted**. Soon after moving in, the children were alone in the house when they heard a moaning noise—like wind making a low, musical whistling sound. These frightening noises continued for several nights, and finally the family decided to investigate. In the basement they discovered a carpenter had left an empty rum bottle in a mortise hole and as the air blew across the bottle neck, the spooky howl was heard throughout the house. •

• • • One needn't always go to rural areas to dig for **buried treasure**. Years ago on what is now Hennessy Street in Halifax, a house stood on a swampy patch of land. Folk history tells us that a man used to come home and hear a voice telling him to search for a treasure in his cellar at midnight. He was to dig until he saw a flag. And like all other treasure digs, he was admonished not to speak while digging or the treasure would sink back into the earth. The man asked a relative to help him dig—they did and found the flag. Unfortunately, his relative was so excited he exclaimed, "Oh lord, there's the flag!" whereupon the flag disappeared and the hole filled with water. Now, there is also a well-known folk belief that, once disturbed, a treasure will not resurface again for seven years. So, unless they dug again seven years later, the treasure is still there. •

• • • Shipbuilders once put **coins under the masts** for good luck. When *Bluenose II* was launched in Lunenburg in 1963, it had a Canadian ten-cent piece, a silver dollar, and a Spanish piece of eight under its main mast, placed there by Colonel Sydney C. Oland, whose family's firm, the popular Nova Scotian brewing company Oland's Limited, commissioned the replica of the famous Grand Banks schooner. On the day Bluenose II slipped into the water, its bow swung around so it was facing the open sea—another good luck omen. •

• • • If you are walking along Brunswick Street in Halifax and hear the faint sound of a tin flute, you may be hearing the residual sounds of a **ghostly musician**. There is a story of a nineteenth-century boy who worked as a musician, playing a penny flute in the taverns that ran along Brunswick Street. The boy disappeared and couldn't be found, but after several years, people began hearing his flute. They searched the area where the music was strongest and found the child's bones beside his flute at the bottom of an abandoned well. They say that after they buried the young musician with his flute the music disappeared—but, who knows? •

• • • In the days of sail, many sailors feared certain actions could cause their vessels to **turn turtle**, as they would say, which meant the ship would capsize or roll over with the bottom of the hull facing upward. Many superstitions were attached to this fear. Cookies or a piece of cake placed upside down on a plate could cause a ship to roll over. In some instances, just holding a cookie or a piece of cake upside down while eating it could have this effect. It was also believed a loaf of bread turned upside down on the table would capsize and sink a ship. •

• • • I remember the days when we had **two-dollar bills**, and even more, when our American neighbours wouldn't accept a two-dollar bill when they visited here. In days gone by, both Americans and some Canadians had reservations concerning the bills—they considered them bad luck. Many fishermen in Nova Scotia called the two-dollar bill a "hoodoo" and wouldn't take one as change back from a purchase. Other folks believed one could change the bad luck by tearing off a tiny piece from one corner. Kind of hard to do with a toonie, but then again, I've never had anyone refuse one either. •

• • • While the occupations of **coal and gold** mining are almost gone in Nova Scotia, when they were in their prime, a number of folk beliefs were attached to them. Many miners felt it was bad luck for a woman to go underground. Some believed that it was bad luck to begin work on a Friday. Others thought it bad luck to tell the day they would retire for fear it would bring on an accident. And some believed in the presence of warnings called "tommy knockers"—tapping sounds underground that foretold of a coming disaster. •

Guysboro Mines Limited Plant, Goldenville, Nova Scotia, 1936.

• • • Have you ever heard of someone having **second sight**? It is a vision of an actual future occurrence. Here's an interesting example from Cape Breton found in the folklore collection of Sister Mary Fraser. An old man named MacNeil of Big Pond was walking along the shore one day when he saw the vision of a body of a man lying on the sand. The corpse was wearing a blue shirt with white buttons and Mr. MacNeil, who had a reputation for having *da-shealladh*—Gaelic for "the two sights"—could also see two women walking toward the corpse. Two years later, a man was out fishing when he took a fit, fell overboard, was drowned, and washed ashore. His body was found by two women in the spot where Mr. MacNeil had seen it before and the drowned man was wearing a blue shirt with white buttons. Now, a fore-runner is something different. It is not the vision of what is to come but some kind of warning of a future event. One such circumstance happened to my great-aunt. She was living in Halifax and her husband was working on a tug boat. One night when he was away, she heard a knock on the door downstairs. She opened the door and there was no one there. However, on the doorstep, she could plainly see a clump of wet seaweed in a pool of water. Next day, she got the call that her husband had drowned. •

• • • If you live in an old house, take a good look at your **doors**. Do they have four or six panels divided by long strips of wood that form the shape of a cross? If so, you have Christian doors. These doors were put in a house to keep out evil forces. An old Nova Scotian folk saying is: "The devil he can fuss and fume, but he can't pass a Christian door!" •

Everyone Complains about the Weather

It's an old adage in Nova Scotia: if you don't like the weather, wait five minutes and it will change.

• • • In 1970, Nova Scotia played host to the world when we were the prime location from which to view a spectacular total **solar eclipse**. The eclipse even made it into the Carly Simon song "You're So Vain," (her lover flies his lear jet to Nova Scotia to witness the event). But Ms. Simon will have to wait a few years more to have cause to write of another such trip. The next total solar eclipse in Nova Scotia will be on April 8, 2024. •

• • • Ok, we have to admit it—Nova Scotia does see its fair share of **fog!** One common folk idiom says, "Fog on the hill, water in the mill; fog in the hollow, fine day tomorrow." At Clark's Harbour, Helen Creighton was told that a "fog breeze" is when the fog blows in from the sea, and a "fog mull" is low-lying fog without wind. But the most common term in this area is "thick o' fog" and my friend Jim Bennet has a great song about it that hits the mark perfectly:

In the fog, thick o'fog,
This North Atlantic weather
Isn't fit for man nor dog.
Through the murky mists that blind us
And the vapours that enwind us
Come and see us (if you can find us)
in the fog.
© Black Rum Music •

• • • Years ago, many individuals kept **weather records** including barometric measurements, rainfall amounts, wind speeds, the arrival of birds, and first sightings of spring and summer plants. It wasn't until the late nineteenth century that we saw the rise

of the science of meteorology. During the nineteenth century, many Nova Scotians relied on the weather predictions in *Belcher's Almanac*. What they didn't know was that these forecasts were probably written by their Justice of the Supreme Court, Jonathan McCully. •

Belcher's Farmer's Almanac, 1825.

• • • Wouldn't it be great if we could **change the weather** at will? Some of the old folk beliefs found in this province say we can. Lay a dead snake belly up and it will rain; whistle and you will bring up the wind, especially at sea. Some homes still have those little weather-houses hanging on the kitchen wall—little plastic houses that resemble a coo-coo clock. Wet weather brings out a pair of old people, while fine weather brings out a pair of children. This weather forecaster was operated by "cat gut" or something similar that reacts to moisture in the air, expanding and contracting to cause the mechanical movements. Ever since I can remember, we had one hanging on our wall at home, and as kids, we used to try and affect the weather by moving them. Sadly, the weather-house is gone now, probably rotted away from the dampness. •

• • • **Weathervanes** were once common fixtures on many buildings in Nova Scotia. The word "vane" comes from the Anglo-Saxon word "fane," meaning "flag." Originally fabric pennants, weather vanes would show the archers the direction of the wind. Later, cloth flags were replaced by metal ones, decorated with the insignia or coat of arms of the lord or nobleman and balanced to turn in the wind...so they should be called wind vanes! Today, they are considered important elements in folk art. The Art Gallery of Nova Scotia has several examples in their collection. The most common style of weathervane features a cockerel, and its use came about by papal decree. In the Gospel of St. Mark, Jesus says to Peter, "before the cock crow twice, thou shalt deny me thrice." To commemorate this statement, in the ninth century Pope Nicholas I ordered that a cockerel should top the highest point of every abbey, cathedral and church in

Christendom. One such Nova Scotian example is the weathervane atop Halifax's Little Dutch Church, once known as "Chicken Cock Church." But perhaps a more regional icon is the salmon weathervane like the one atop the Anglican church in Sherbrooke (which is a match for one I saw atop a church in Sneem, Ireland). And one of this province's most famous weathervanes towers over historic St. George's Anglican Church in Halifax. It features an image of Halley's Comet added in 1835 in recognition of that celestial body's appearance. •

Old Dutch Church, Halifax, circa 1890, showing weathervane cockerel.

• • • I can remember my grandparents listening to the radio to hear "the probs" ("probabilities")—the term they used for the **weather forecast**. Although they relied upon forecasts given over the radio and in the newspaper, years of experience had also taught them to heed the natural elements themselves. I often heard "big snow, little snow," meaning if the first flakes begin big there will be little snow and it may turn to rain, but if the flakes are tiny and fluffy a big snowstorm can be expected. And at Halifax, Helen Creighton collected this weather rhyme:

**"Snow like meal, snow a great deal;
snow like feathers, softening weather."** •

• • • Next time it snows and you're waiting for the plow, just be grateful you're not **warned out** as in times gone by. For many years, men were required to give a certain amount of time to road work in lieu of, or in addition to, taxes. After a storm an official would "warn out" the workers to clear public roads. And to make it even more difficult, you were expected to shovel the road surface leaving a skim of snow—that way the runners of the sleighs could run easily over the surface without scraping on gravel. •

• • • The pre-contact **Mi'kmaq** used the natural resources of the land to their best use. They lived by the shore from late spring to the fall and moved inland in winter for warmth and to track large game. However, they did acknowledge a lean period for food gathering and hunting. Early spring made overland travel difficult and the ice too risky to move about on. The people relied on dried and smoked foods to get them through what they called "starving time." •

• • • Ok, I'll concede that we often have winters during which we have just cause to complain about the weather. The huge **snow storm** we had in 2004, called White Juan in recognition of the previous fall's Hurricane Juan, had the entire province shut down for days and was the cause of many complaints. But, hey, complaining about our weather is nothing new. In 1788, William Dyott was a young garrison officer posted to Halifax who complained bitterly about what he called the "cold, nasty weather." He lamented that it kept him indoors with nothing to do but play cards and eat and drink. And he also lamented, as we still do today, "It is impossible to depend on the weather for twenty-four hours in this country." •

• • • One of the earliest references to **hurricanes** in Nova Scotia was in 1635. On August 15 of that year, a hurricane swept the Eastern Seaboard. One of the fiercest storms to hit our province—known appropriately as The Great Storm—came on September 25, 1798. Titus Smith (sometimes referred to as Nova Scotia's first ecologist) mentioned it in his memoirs. He recalled how difficult it was to travel through the devastated forests, saying he was "obliged to spend a half hour in going 100 yards" through the deadwood. This storm was also noted by Thomas Chandler Haliburton, who wrote, "A dreadful storm and gale of wind at Halifax, by which shipping, wharves and other property was destroyed. Most of the roads were impassable from the falling of forest trees." Simeon Perkins, the famous diarist from Liverpool, noted that "the tide was very high and Liverpool was heavily damaged…all the trees and potatoes and many other things appeared black as if hit by a frost." •

• • • My earliest **hurricane memory** is of Edna, which arrived on September 11, 1954, and caused considerable damage. Edna brought hundred-mile-an-hour winds that took power and phone lines down. The apple crop in the Annapolis Valley was more than ninety percent ruined. Barns were blown down, animals killed, and at least one human was crushed by falling buildings. The Shelburne Yacht Club was destroyed. More than two decades later, Hurricane Blanche hit on July 28, 1975, and although Blanche tore an oil rig off its moorings in Halifax Harbour and stranded it on the Dartmouth shore, narrowly missing the A. Murray Mackay bridge, Edna still held the record for the most damage recorded in Nova Scotia—that is, until Juan hit. Then all hell broke loose and the old records were shattered. •

Damage from Hurricane Juan, Halifax, 2003.

Bibliography

Avis, Walter S., editor. *Dictionary of Canadianisms on Historical Principles.* Toronto: W.J. Gage Limited, 1967.

Backhouse, Constance. "Racial Segregation in Canadian Legal History: Viola Desmond's Challenge, Nova Scotia, 1946." *Dalhousie Law Journal.* Vol. 17, #2, 1994.

Bagnell, Kenneth. *The Little Immigrants: The Orphans Who Came to Canada.* Toronto: Macmillan of Canada, 1980.

Barss, Peter and Joleen Gordon. *Older Ways: Traditional Nova Scotian Craftsmen.* Toronto: Van Nostrand Reinhold, 1980.

Baterman, Jack, and others. *The World of Games.* New York: Facts on File, 1989.

Belmore, Eleanor M. *Caribou Gold Mines 1865-1990.* Privately published, 1990.

A.B. Bennet & Garnet Heislor. *Duelling Dories: 50 Years of International Dory Racing in Nova Scotia.* Tantallon: Glen Margaret Publishing, 2002.

Bennet, Jim. *Thick O'Fog.* Black Rum Music; used with permission.

Bird, Will R. *This is Nova Scotia.* Philadelphia: Macrea Smith and Co., 1950.

Bishop, Jennie. "Seafaring Maiden." *Family Herald.* November 7 1957.

Bishop, Tony. *Gold Hunters Guide to Nova Scotia.* Halifax: Nimbus, 1988.

Bjarnasonand, Johann Magnus. Trans. Lawrence Gillespie. *Eirikus Hansson: An Icelandic Boy's Adventures in Nova Scotia.* Unpublished manuscript, NSARM.

Blakeley, Phyllis R. *Two Remarkable Giants.* Windsor: Lancelot Press, 1970.

Borrett, William C. *Down East: And Other Cargo of Tales Told Under the Old Town Clock.* Halifax: The Imperial Publishing Company, 1945.

Brebner, John Bartlet. *The Neutral Yankees of Nova Scotia.* Toronto: McClelland and Stewart, 1969.

Bridgland, A. S., editor. *The Modern Tailor, Outfitter and Clothier.* The Claxton Publishing Company, 1936.

Byers, Mary and Margaret McBurney. *Atlantic Hearth: Early Homes and Families of Nova Scotia.* Toronto: University of Toronto Press, 1994.

Campbell, Mavis C. *Back to Africa: George Ross and the Maroons, from Nova Scotia to Sierra Leone.* Trenton, New Jersey: Africa World Press, 1993.

Carrigan, D. Owen. *Crime and Punishment in Canada: A History*. Toronto: McClelland & Stewart, 1991.

Chiasson, Father Anselme, editor. *The History of Cheticamp Hooked Rugs and Their Artisans*. Yarmouth: Lescarbot, 1988.

Choyce, Lesley, editor. *Alternating Currents: Renewable Energy for Atlantic Canada*. Halifax: Wooden Anchor Press,1977.

Clark, S.D. *The Social Development of Canada*. Toronto: University of Toronto Press, 1942.

Collins, Louis W. *In Halifax Town*. Halifax: Privately printed, 1975.

Cook, Francis. *Introduction to Canadian Amphibians and Reptiles*. Ottawa: National Museum of Natural Sciences, 1984.

Comeau, F.G.J. "The Origin and History of the Apple Industry in Nova Scotia." *Nova Scotia Historical Society*. Volume 23, 1936.

Christie, Barbara J. "The Morgan Horse in Nova Scotia." *The Occasional*. Volume 9, Number 1, Fall 1984.

Creighton, Helen. *A Folk Tale Journey Through the Maritimes*. Eds. Michael Taft and Ronald Caplan. Wreck Cove: Breton Books, 1993.

____. *Bluenose Ghosts* Toronto. Ryerson, 1957.

____. *Bluenose Magic: Popular Beliefs and Superstitions in Nova Scotia*. Toronto: Ryerson, 1968.

____. *Folklore of Lunenburg County, Nova Scotia*. Toronto: McGraw-Hill Ryerson, 1976. [reprint of the National Museum of Canada Bulletin Number 117, Anthropological Series Number 29, 1950. Author's additions to second edition]

Croft, Clary. "Helen Creighton: Collecting the German-based Folklore of Lunenburg County, Nova Scotia." *German-Canadian Yearbook*, Volume 16, Toronto, 2000.

____. *Chocolates, Tattoos and Mayflowers: Mainstreet Memorabilia from Clary Croft*. Halifax: Nimbus, 1995.

Cunningham, Robert. *Tidewrack*. Hantsport: Lancelot Press, 1994.

Davis, Stephen A. *The Micmac: People of the Maritimes*. Tantallon: Four East Publications, 1991.

____. Catherine Cottreau and Laird Niven. *Artifacts from Eighteenth Century Halifax*. Halifax: Saint Mary's University Archeology Laboratory, 1987.

Degler, Teri. *Scuttlebutt: And Other Expressions of Nautical Origin*. Saskatoon: Western Producer Prairie Books, 1989.

Dennis, Clara. *Down In Nova Scotia*. Toronto: The Ryerson Press, 1934.

____. *More About Nova Scotia*. Toronto: The Ryerson Press, 1937.

Denys, Nicolas. "Concerning the Ways of the Indians: their customs, dress, methods of hunting and fishing, and their amusements." First published in French in 1672. Nova Scotia Department of Education, n/d.

Donovan, Kenneth. "Louisbourg Gaming." *Canadian Collector*. March/April 1985.

Ells, Margaret. "The Dartmouth Whalers." *The Dalhousie Review*. Vol. 15, #1, 1975.

Farnham, C.H. "Cape Breton Folk." *Harpers' New Monthly Magazine*. Volume 72, December 1885 to May 1886.

Fauset, Arthur Huff. "Folklore from Nova Scotia" *American Folklore Society*. Volume 24, 1931

Feldman, David. *When Did Wild Poodles Roam the Earth?* New York: HarperCollins, 1992.

Fergusson, C. Bruce. "Jewish Communities in Nova Scotia" *Nova Scotia Journal of Education* Volume 11, #1, 1961.

____. "The Floral Emblem of Nova Scotia." *Nova Scotia Historical Quarterly* Volume 4, #1, March 1974.

____. H.A. Innis & D.C. Harvey, editors. *The Diary of Simeon Perkins*. Toronto: Champlain Society, 1948-58.

Fingard, Judith, Janet Guilford, David Sutherland. *Halifax: The First 250 Years*. Halifax: Formac, 1999.

Franklin, John H. *From Slavery to Freedom: A History of Negro Americans*. New York: Vintage Books, 1969.

Fraser, Mary. *Folklore of Nova Scotia*. Antigonish: Formac, 1975. (Reprint)

Friends of the Public Gardens. *The Halifax Public Gardens*. Halifax: Friends of the Public Gardens, 1989.

Furlong, Pauline. *Historic Amherst*. Halifax: Nimbus, 2001.

Gilhen, John. *Amphibians and Reptiles of Nova Scotia*. Halifax: Nova Scotia Museum, 1984.

Glimpses in and about Halifax, Nova Scotia. Published by W. H. Howard, 1896.

Goeb, Jan. *The Maritime Jewish Community*. Halifax: Halifax Jewish Historical Society, c.1975.

Grant, John. "Early Blacks of Nova Scotia." *Nova Scotia Journal of Education* Volume 5, Fall, 1977.

____. *The Maroons in Nova Scotia*. Halifax: Formac, 2002.

Grantmyre, Barbara. "The Canal that Bisected Nova Scotia." *Canadian Geographical Journal* Volume 88, Number 1, January, 1974.

Green, Lorne. *Life of a Nation Builder—Sanford Fleming*. Dundurn Press, 1994.

Halifax and Its People 1749-1999: Images from Nova Scotia Archives and Record Management Halifax: Nimbus & Nova Scotia Archives and Record Management, 1999.

Hamilton, William. *The Nova Scotia Traveller: A Maritimer's Guide to His Home Province*. Longman Trade/Caroline House, 1985.

Hartling, Phillip. *Where Broad Atlantic Surges Roar*. Antigonish: Formac, 1979.

Harvey, D.C. "Nova Scotia and the Canadian Naval Tradition." *Canadian Historical Review* Volume 23. Toronto: University of Toronto Press, 1942.

Hattie, W.H. "Early Acadian Hospitals." *Journal of the Canadian Medical Association* Volume 16, 1926.

Jobes, Gerturde. *Dictionary of Mythology, Folklore and Symbols*. New York: The Scarecrow Press, 1962.

Johnston, Keith. "Drink Trade in Halifax 1870—1895". B.A. Hon. Thesis, Dalhousie University, 1977.

Julien, Donald. *Historical Perspective of Micmac Indians pre & Post Contact Period*. Research paper prepared for the Confederacy of Mainland Micmac, c.1988.

Kallman, Helmut. *A History of Music in Canada 1534-1914*. Toronto: University of Toronto Press 1960.

Kingsbury, Al. *The Pumpkin King: Howard Dill and the Atlantic Giant*. Hantsport: Lancelot Press, 1992.

Kipling, Rudyard. *Captains Courageous*. New York: F. Watts, c.1898.

Kitz, Janet F. *Shattered City: The Halifax Explosion and the Road to Recovery*. Halifax: Nimbus, 1989.

Klink, Carl F. *Literary History of Canada*. Toronto: University of Toronto Press, c.1965.

Knockwood, Noel. "Mythology and Religion of the Micmac People." *Social Services News* Halifax, Nova Scotia: Department of Social Services, 1975.

Lamb, James B. *The Celtic Crusader*. Hantsport: Lancelot Press, 1992.

Lavoie, Marc C. "Archaeological Evidence of Planter Material Culture in New Brunswick and Nova Scotia." Ed. Margaret Conrad. *Making Changes: Change and Continuity in Planter Nova Scotia 1759-1800*. Fredericton: Acadiensis Press, 1991.

Lawson, Mrs. William. *History of the Townships of Dartmouth, Preston and Lawerencetown* Belleville, Ontario: Mika Studios, 1972. [originally published in 1893 by Morton and Company, Halifax. Facsimile edition edited by Harry Piers]

Leach, Maria, ed. *Standard Dictionary of Folklore, Mythology, and Legend*. 2 volumes New York: Funk and Wagnalls, 1949-1950.

Lindal, W.J. *The Icelanders in Canada*. Ottawa: National Publishers, 1967.

Lock, Carolyn. *Country Colors: A Guide to Natural Dyeing in Nova Scotia*. Halifax: Nova Scotia Museum, 1981.

MacKenzie, Michael. *Tracks Across the Maritimes*. Christmas Island: MacKenzie Books, 1985.

Maclean, Hugh. *Man of Steel: The Story of Sir Sanford Fleming*. Toronto: Ryerson Press, 1969.

Maestro, Maria Erie. *The Chinese in Nova Scotia: An Overview and a Preliminary Bibliography*. Halifax: School of Library and Information Studies, Dalhousie University, 1992.

Marble, Allan E. *Surgeons, Smallpox, and the Poor: A History of Medicine and Social Conditions in Nova Scotia 1749-1799*. Montreal: McGill-Queen's University Press, 1993.

Martin, John P. *The Story of Dartmouth*. Dartmouth: Privately printed, 1957.

Maynard, Kimberley Smith, Philip Girard, Jim Philips, editors. "Divorce in Nova Scotia 1750-1890." *Essays in the History of Canadian Law*, Volume 111, Toronto: University of Toronto Press, 1990.

McCurdy, William H. *The MacKay Motor Car: Nova Scotia's First*. privately published, 1967.

Milks, Robert E. *75 Years of scouting in Canada*. Ottawa: Scouts Canada, 1982.

Myers, J.C. *Sketches of a Town through the Northern and Eastern States, The Canadas and Nova Scotia*. Harrisonburg: J.H. Wartmann and Brothers, 1849.

Myers, Jay. *Canadian Facts and Dates*. Fitzhenry & Whiteside.

Newton, Pamela. *The Cape Breton Book of Days*. Sydney: University College of Cape Breton Press, 1984.

Nickerson, Roger. "The Nova Scotia Tartan: An Update." *Nova Scotia Historical Review* Volume 11, #2, 1991.

Parker, Mike. *Guides of the North Woods*. Halifax: Nimbus, 1990.

_____. *Historic Lunenburg: The Days of Sail 1880-1930*. Halifax: Nimbus, 1999.

Parsons, Elsie Clew. "Micmac Folklore." *Journal of American Folklore* Volume 38, 1925.

_____. "Micmac Notes" *Journal of American Folklore* Volume 39, 1926.

Pettigrew, Eileen. *The Silent Enemy: Canadian and the Deadly Flu of 1918*. Western Producer Prairie Books, 1983.

Poirier, Leonie Comeau. *My Acadian Heritage*. Hantsport: Lancelot Press, 1985.

Poteet, Lewis J. *The South Shore Phrase Book*. Hantsport: Lancelot Press, 1983.

_____. *The Second South Shore Phrase Book*. Hantsport: Lancelot Press, 1985.

Raddall, Thomas Head. *Halifax: Warden of the North*. Garden City, N. Y. : Doubleday, 1965.

Rand, Silas T. *Legends of the Micmacs*. New York and London: Longmans, Green, and Company, 1894.

Rankin, D. J. *A History of the County of Antigonish, Nova Scotia* Toronto: The Macmillan Company Canada Limited, 1929.

Reader's Digest Facts and Fallacies New York and Montreal: The Reader's Digest Association, 1988.

Reynolds, Ted. ed. *That's A Good Question, Canada!* Calgary: Script: The Writers' Group, 1990.

Robertson, Marion. *The Chestnut Pipe: Folklore of Shelburne County*. Halifax: Nimbus, 1991.

Robinson, John and Thomas Rispin. *Journey through Nova-Scotia Containing A Particular Account of the Country and its Inhabitants. 1774*. Sackville: Ralph Pickard Bell Library, Mount Allison University, 1981.

Rubinger, Catherine. "Marriage and the Women of Louisbourg". *Dalhousie Review* Volume 60, #3, 1980.

Salter, Michael. "L'Ordre de Bon Temps." *Nova Scotia Historical Quarterly* Volume 5, #2, 1975.

Sanders Garner, Betty. *Canada's Monsters*. Hamilton: Potlatch Publications, 1976.

Sheppard, Tom. *Historic Queens County, Nova Scotia*. Halifax: Nimbus, 2001.

Sherwood, Roland H. *The Brides' Ship: And Other Tales of the Unusual*. Hantsport: Lancelot Press, 1990.

Shyu, Larry N. *The Chinese: Peoples of the Maritimes*. Halifax: Nimbus, 1997.

Sinclair, D. MacLean. "Gaelic in Nova Scotia." *Dalhousie Review* Volume 30, 1950.

Spicer, Stanley T. *Maritimers Ashore and Afloat*. Hantsport: Lancelot Press, 1994.

Taylor, Lou. *Mourning Dress: A Costume and Social History*. London: George Allen and Unwin, 1983.

Thompson, Chai-Chu. "Chinese Community of Halifax-Dartmouth Area." *Your World*: *International Education Centre Newsletter*, Volume 3, #1, 1981.

Trider, Douglas William. *The History of the Dartmouth Quakers*. Hantsport: Lancelot, 1985.

Waring, Phillipa. *A Dictionary of Omens and Superstitions*. London: Souvenir Press, 1978.

Whitehead, Ruth Holmes. *The Old Man Told Us: Excerpts from Micmac History 1500-1950*. Halifax: Nimbus, 1991.

_____. and Harold McGee. *The Micmac: How Their Ancestors Lived Five Hundred Years Ago*. Halifax: Nimbus, 1983.

Photo credits

Barbara Miller Manning Collection: 18
Clary Croft Collection: 64, 71, 79, 92
Croft, Clary: 2, 6, 26, 33(left), 37(bottom left), 50, 61(bottom left), 78, 86, 87, 90(right), 98, 99
Croft, Sharon: 25(left), 29, 65(right)
Cumberland County Museum Collection: 56
Dartmouth Heritage Museum Society: 3(left), 20(right), 21, 27, 35, 40, 41,49(right), 52, 54, 55, 57, 65(left), 67(left), 68(left), 101, 106
Don and Marjorie Campagna Collection: 37(top left), 45, 66
Don Snider Collection, courtesy of Marie MacGillivray: 39

Howard Dill Collection: 49(left)
Maritime Museum of the Atlantic: 24
Middleton, Rodger: 37(right)
National Archives of Canada: 8(left), 8(right)
Nova Scotia Archives and Record Management: 3(right), 5, 7, 10, 12, 13, 15, 17, 19, 20 (left), 22, 23, 25(right), 30, 31, 32, 33(right), 34, 38, 42, 44, 48, 58, 59, 60, 61(top), 64, 67, 68(right), 69, 72, 75, 80, 84, 85, 88, 89, 90(left), 91, 94, 95, 105.
Olive and Clarence Croft Collection: 103
Secord, Carol: 108
W.L. Bishop Collection: 93